JONESTOWN SURVIVOR

An Insider's Look

Laura Johnston Kohl

iUniverse, Inc.

New York Bloomington

Jonestown Survivor
An Insider's Look

Copyright © 2010 Laura Johnston Kohl

iUniverse books may be ordered through booksellers or by contacting:

iUniverse
1663 Liberty Drive
Bloomington, IN 47403
www.iuniverse.com
1-800-Authors (1-800-288-4677)

ISBN: 978-1-4502-2094-1 (pbk)
ISBN: 978-1-4502-2096-5 (cloth)
ISBN: 978-1-4502-2095-8 (ebk)

Printed in the United States of America

iUniverse rev. date: 3/15/2010

I dedicate this book to my friends from Peoples Temple—
those who did and those who did not survive. We
united to help improve this world for all people.

SPECIAL ACKNOWLEDGEMENTS

My "Rs": my husband, Ron, and our son, Raul, have supported me endlessly and deeply to find peace with my past and continue my search for clarity. My mother, Virginia, a survivor, teacher, and author, inspired me and gave me strength to meet the challenges I have faced. My sister, Linda, continues to give me encouragement and love every day. My fellow Peoples Temple members have brought me the greatest joy and love. For those who survived, I cannot imagine my life without you. For those who live only in my memory, it is you who compel me to tell our story.

I could never have completed this work without consistent expert advice and help from my village of friends, especially: Fielding McGehee, Rebecca Moore, my sister Linda, Sonja Eriksson, Kiki Dulaney, Chris Downing, Roena Oesting, Laurie Leyne, Garry Lambrev, Leslie Wilson, Tim Carter, Don Beck, Elena Broslovsky, and Janet Lynch. Thank you.

Contents

Introduction   xi

Chapter 1   Who Am I?   1

Chapter 2   Biding My Time   6

Chapter 3   College Days   16

Chapter 4   What is Peoples Temple?   25

Chapter 5   What Were We Planning?   44

Chapter 6   My First Trip to Paradise-1974   58

Chapter 7   A Tropical Destination   62

Chapter 8   Georgetown and Survival   71

Chapter 9   Leaving My Home in Guyana   81

Chapter 10   Another Community Steps In-Synanon   89

Chapter 11   Placing One Foot in Front of the Other   98

Chapter 12   All Alone in a Big World   104

Chapter 13   My Heart Was Filled Again   110

Chapter 14   Friends, My Dear Friends   122

Chapter 15   And What is on the Horizon?   132

Who Survived the Jonestown Tragedy?   137

Who Died in Guyana on November 18, 1978?   143

Introduction

This book is about my life, from the beginning to this day. It began in such a mild and uncomplicated way. There was no clue about the tsunamis I would face.

My early life was rather ordinary. I was an activist with a politically savvy mother. From the first moment I arrived at college, I was on a quest to discover what I was all about. The next years took me to Woodstock, to the Black Panthers, to Peoples Temple and inexplicably out of Jonestown, then into Synanon, into marriage, parenting, teaching, and the Quaker religion.

I am a composite of all of these experiences.

I speak only for myself. I share my life as I understand it today. My reflections about and understanding of my experiences continue to evolve. I am not interested in arguing who I was or who I am. I can only be who I am and, these days, I am content with that. I am a curious person. I am determined to uncover more about my experiences, particularly about Peoples Temple, more than I knew at the time I lived it.

I am writing about my life before, during, and after Peoples Temple. I was a member for ten years. Although roughly only one-sixth of my life, it has affected every part of me. I am a very different person because of my Peoples Temple experience.

Peoples Temple did not begin or die on November 18, 1978, even though much of the media coverage and general information focuses on that day.

Many of the folks who loved Jonestown and Guyana died there, so they are not able to tell you their side of the story.

We read about those who wanted to leave, those who didn't find their niche, and those who saw Jim Jones for the madman he became (despite Jim's best efforts to keep his insanity well hidden). Some survived and have told their stories. These represent one side of the Peoples Temple story.

There is no way to minimize the outcome. There is no way to deny that 918 loving and loved people died for no good reason. There is no way to forget or to excuse that but for being with Jim Jones in Guyana in Peoples Temple at that moment in time, they would die.

There is simply more to the story. Love, fellowship and good intentions were the glue that we shared in Peoples Temple.

Are there universal truths about Peoples Temple? I do not know. What I do know is that I have never believed in heaven or hell. I believe my own eyes – what I see on a day-to-day basis in my own life and around the world.

When I flew into Guyana to join my friends in Peoples Temple, I was immediately enthralled and believed I might have found the "promised land." I loved the rich colors of the Guyanese people, from coal black to light beige, like me. I loved their accents. I loved that people of different ethnic backgrounds lived harmoniously with each other in Guyana (Afro American, Chinese, AmerIndian, East Indian and more). I loved that citizens elected government representatives from among many ethnic groups. I saw and felt no racism as I interacted with the Guyanese. I saw and felt a richness and depth in the fabric of the country. I was in love with Guyana from the first moment.

My story doesn't stop there, because I didn't stop. I couldn't. This book follows me through my survival. I often meet people and give them a glimpse of my life. They are inevitably astounded. At first glance, I look like them, or their sisters, or their neighbor. I don't wear my battle scars outwardly, but I certainly do carry them inside.

CHAPTER I
Who Am I?

My early history was probably much like your early history. No fortune teller could have guessed my future.

My mom, Virginia Richardson Reid, grew up in Pittsburgh, Pennsylvania. She was raised by her widowed mother, Mabel. She attended and graduated from Bethany College in West Virginia. She was told she had the highest IQ of any of Bethany's freshmen. She majored in journalism.

My father, John Bryan Reid, grew up in Birmingham, Alabama and Miami Beach, Florida. He was an athletic boy – a runner, wrestler, and boxer. In 1934, at the age of fifteen, he contracted polio. His muscles wasted and he was wheelchair-bound because his leg muscles were not able to support his body. His weight fell to less than 100 pounds. His family and he were told that he should "take it easy" because he was going to be "a cripple" for life. Somehow he came to believe that he could rebuild his body through weight lifting and band stretching and he threw himself into a grueling, painful regime of exercise, exercise, exercise – all from his wheelchair. My father built himself up to being an actual poster boy for the magazine *Strength & Health*. By 1940, he claimed to have been considered one of the strongest men in America. He put himself through correspondence school to become a certified public accountant and later wrote a pamphlet for other aspiring CPAs – "*What Every Young Accountant Should Know.*"

My mother was a green-eyed beauty and a bit on the anxious side.

My father was tall, dark, and handsome with a great sense of humor. My parents met in Washington, DC, where my father worked in the accounting field and my mom was a writer. They married shortly after they met – North meets South on the Mason Dixon line.

I was born on October 22, 1947, in Washington, D.C., at George Washington Hospital, the youngest of three daughters. My father yearned to return to the South, so soon after I was born, our family moved from DC to Dallas, Texas. Two years later, my parents separated. My sisters and I left Texas with Mom and went to Pittsburgh to live with my grandmother, Nana. My father stayed in Texas, started a new family and lived there the rest of his life.

I don't remember living in Texas or having my father in the home at all. After my parents' divorce, I only remember my mom crying a lot and being very unhappy for many years. She retained a lifelong resentment against my father, Texas, his new family and anyone mentioning any of those topics. I don't recall missing my father's presence in my life. I had never been accustomed to it. I think my older sisters were more affected by his absence.

Divorce in the late 1940s was unusual. Mom claimed that Nana was ashamed of her when we returned to Pittsburgh from Texas. Divorced women were almost unheard of in suburban communities – the places where kids were supposed to be raised. At that time, college-educated women and working women were also odd ducks. Mom had domestic responsibilities, but the life of the mind was her true passion. Divorce gave her the chance to find the kind of personal freedom most women did not have in those days. It also embittered her.

Mom went job hunting in DC while we stayed with Nana. Soon after she secured a job and rented an apartment, she came and got us. We moved to New Alexandria, Virginia. She found work as a ghostwriter of political speeches and an assistant for Pennsylvania Senator James H. Duff. She once wrote a speech for John Kennedy on water-based electrical power, such as that generated by Hoover Dam. Later, she worked as an editor for the American Public Power Association magazine. Late in her life, she obtained a Ford Foundation scholarship and went back to school to obtain her teaching credential, agreeing to teach in the Washington DC public school system. She retired from teaching and continued as an activist, taking her grandchildren with her to picket the White House on public interest issues.

As a beautiful, brilliant divorcee with three young daughters, her drive and the single life gave her the opportunity to open new doors for women – at least the three who lived with her. She bought a house in Rockville, Maryland, and moved us to suburbia. Her wide interests led her to expose us to theater, travel, art, politics and other virginal explorations – all without a hint of male presence. She became President of the Parent-Teacher Association, she was a member of the Rockville Planning Commission, and she was a block leader for the Democratic Party. Work, work, work. As soon as she was able to convince Nana to give up her life in Pittsburgh, Mom had Nana come and live with us. Nana was the typical "woman of the house" in suburbia – baking cookies, gossiping with the neighbors, reading picture-oriented magazines. Mom was the "man of the house" – working long hours, being exasperated at the trivial interests of Nana, etc. The main difference was that at work, as a woman, Mom had all of the responsibilities and about 1/3 of the pay of the drunkard who held the official title reflecting the work that Mom did. And, of course, she had to endure being told how "lucky" she was to have a job other than secretary or receptionist, the only jobs most women were considered for in those days.

My father, the epitome of the southern "good ole boy," became a successful CPA, wrote a column on life insurance taxation for *Best's Review*, served as an expert witness in accounting cases, and wrote books on accounting issues and on self-improvement topics. His new family somehow merged into my family, mainly through the efforts of his great wife, Barbara. Barbara, a "my house is your house" beacon of love, has loved us and made sure that we are one big family, all of us. Our relationship with our father (whom we called "Jack" and his new family called "John") was distant and periodic. He did call and send child support checks. We received Christmas and birthday gifts, but we rarely saw him. He attended neither graduations nor weddings. He would show up unexpectedly. I remember a visit when I was in junior high school. He visited us in Rockville and challenged my boyfriend, George, to tear a phone book in half with his bare hands. George couldn't do it, but Jack could. He was delighted that he could challenge a strong young kid and win. Perhaps because he had been so incapacitated by polio during puberty, he initiated a life-long competition with any other man or boy he met. As a Dad, at a distance, I could appreciate him more and more as I got older.

I come from several generations of single-mom females —my mother, my grandmother, my great-grandmother and perhaps further back than three generations. My great grandmother, Nellie McNerney, worked on an Army base in Kansas, where my grandmother was born. Not much is known about Nellie's husband, except that he was not a part of Nellie and Nana's life. Nana married Charles Richardson, and my mother was conceived shortly after that. Charles died when my Mom was 6 months old. Family lore is that he died of cancer, but the records indicate that he died from tuberculosis (a disease as shameful as AIDS used to be considered). And, of course, Mom, who was a single mom with three daughters, aged 2, 4 and 6.

My great-grandmother had no formal education. My grandmother left school after the 8th grade. My mother graduated from college and, in her 60s, obtained her Masters Degree in education. Each woman was independent, strong-minded and adventurous. Each daughter, in her own way, had anger issues with her mother. Each daughter brought her mother forward into the future with her as a helpmate, until my generation. My grandmother had been kicked out of the Catholic Church because Charles refused to raise my mom as a Catholic. She became a high Episcopalian, turned Methodist, and was a long-time Republican. My mother was kicked out of the Episcopalian Church because of her divorce, developed a disinterest in religious institutions and became something of a religious cynic.

Being responsible for the futures of three young daughters, she was frightened by the atmosphere of fear in DC during the McCarthy period of the early 1950s. She had joined the professional alliance called The Newspaper Guild, which was one of the many harmless organizations made to appear sinister by Senator Joseph McCarthy. She was committed to the principles of our country, but fearful as the sole supporter of our family during this dangerous time.

Our family didn't have much of a support system. My grandmother and my mother were both only children. My father and his family lived in Texas. Our other distant relatives were scattered far away. We had a cousin in Scituate, Massachusetts, who lived an alternative life style with her friend, Helen. We spent many summers visiting them.

Mom frequently took us to the city of her dreams, New York. We would go to Coney Island, see plays, and take the Long Island Ferry and see the sights. It seems like we spent a lot of time driving north to New Jersey, New York and Massachusetts, just for the adventure of travel and because driving was the least expensive way to go. I guess we three kids were rascals of an innocuous sort, sometimes reading during our travels and sometimes not. My sister, Linda, and I would sometimes moon the car behind us on these drives. We also threw notes out of our car window that said "Help Us! We are being kidnapped!" or "Please adopt us. We don't belong with this woman." Our family dynamic was two against two – with Linda and me usually opposing my mother and sister Ellen.

Politics aside, we were comfortable and unobtrusive in our lives in Rockville. We had sibling rivalry, homework issues, broken legs, emergency appendectomies, lost and found cat sagas, and bad hair days. We were a family, but an unusual one for that day and time because of the absence of any male mammal in the household. Even our cats and dogs were always female.

Chapter 2
Biding My Time

Our neighborhood in Rockville was called "Twinbrook." It was a planned community with a community pool and clubhouse, but a lower middle class community with electricians, businessmen, repairmen and housewives. It was an all-white, picket-fence type of community, but integrated on the junior high and high school level prior to the Supreme Court ruling. There were black neighborhoods. None of the city business or government buildings had segregated areas. Tough in many ways Maryland was a southern city at the time, blacks were an everyday presence in our lives even though they were not our nearby neighbors.

Because divorce was so alien to that environment, my mother certainly stood out but was not to be thwarted. She developed her deepest friendships around politics and city government. She was an active, street-walking Democrat, and also an appointed member of the Rockville Planning Commission for many years. Our elementary school was a half-block from our door. For a while, my mother paid a neighbor to watch us before and after school. There were constant interruptions from home while Mom was at work. I remember one frenzied call I made to her at her job when our cat rushed in our open front door, followed by a neighbor's large dog, running around and around inside our house. Being a single parent, working an hour away from home, and having three feisty young daughters was very difficult for Mom.

I can only imagine how isolated and frightened she must have felt with no support network, living in the suburbs. There was nothing "suburban" about Mom. She made many sacrifices for us and worked very hard at being the best parent she could be. As an only child, her childhood had been very lonely. She told us she had dreamed of having a sister to love. I think she idealized motherhood and expected that it would heal her loneliness, only to find that sibling rivalry was a kind of hell for someone raised as an only child. The clash of her expectations with her real life led her to overreact to situations that others might let pass.

As we all do, she tried to correct parenting errors she believed her own mother had committed. She was raised with the standard of her day that "children should be seen and not heard." My mother had to nurture herself to get through school, go to college and seek a career. She did this through her intellectual pursuits. She fought and won the battle to be true to herself. What she accomplished just was not done in my grandmother's society, where men were expected to continue their education and get jobs, but women were not to do so.

My mother and my grandmother were worlds apart in interests, in philosophies and in temperaments. They were one as to devotion to children and grandchildren and each would have done anything within her power to help her child.

Nana moved down from Pittsburgh so that she could be home for us when we got out of school. She spoiled me rotten. She was loving and kind and had a fabulous sense of humor. Her eyes would twinkle when she shared jokes and she loved to poke fun at herself. I remember when she told the family that she might just switch her vote from Eisenhower to Adlai Stevenson (as Mom urged her to do) because she had had a naughty dream about Adlai and herself. From that point on, whenever Adlai's name was mentioned, she feigned a love swoon. Hilarious.

Nana and I had a very special bond. Nana loved soap operas. For her, "news" was the latest development on *As the World Turns*. In some ways, I guess the soap gave her a glimpse of the complex life she may have lived on her own, as an unmarried professional women in Pittsburgh. She had left that life behind to come and rescue Mom and us, but the yearning remained.

Nana would look forward to Mom coming home from work so that she could have adult conversation. Mom would come in exhausted from her work days of responsibility without commensurate pay or respect. It was a daily battle—Nana seeking closeness with her daughter; Mom seeking distance, peace and quiet. Nana's recitation of the daily soap opera shenanigans generally ignited Mom's explosive post-work temper. So often my mother would lose patience with Nana and lash out. Nana would go crying to her room. They were as different as a rock and a sponge. Nana's clear priority was Mom. Mom's last priority was Nana's isolation and companionship needs. Mom seemed to hate that she needed Nana to keep our lives together, but we all knew how interdependent they were.

Nana gave us a warm, gentle and quaint family life. Mom introduced us to the wider world of travel, politics, theater, music, dance, literature and social issues.

The artist in me, as seen by Mom, was a budding ballerina and violinist, pianist and/or accordion player. Thus, Mom sent me to ballet lessons for many years, bought me a violin and signed me up for violin lessons. My violinist career was cut short by the unwillingness of my family to tolerate the screech of my assigned instrument. Or perhaps the instructor advised that I was not a prodigy. I remember nothing of this experience except how funny it seems in retrospect—me and a violin! Ballet was a different matter. My teacher lived in our neighborhood and was inspirational. She and her husband were dancers with the Washington Ballet Company. Our ballet class held recitals and I learned the music for many lovely ballets. Sometimes our recitals were held in a Rockville auditorium and dancers from the Washington Ballet Company would perform with us. My painful modesty compelled me to quit ballet (developing breasts + leotard = (to me) naked body). Perhaps Mom thought ballet might help me overcome my modesty. I remember being somewhat clumsy before the ballet lessons taught me about positioning and movement. In any event, I have happy memories of how I often avoided practicing (sprains, colds, and malaise) and loved performing, even though grace is not one of my natural talents.

My elementary school offered a pilot program to teach youngsters how to speak Spanish. I took the program in third grade. My teacher and the subject inspired my love of the people and the language and led to further study in high school (2 Latin classes & 3 Spanish classes) and college to become fluent in Spanish. The love affair begun with that elementary school class has continued to this day

Our twelve years in Rockville were predictable and safe. We were model residents and lived a traditional lifestyle. I believe we were the only family headed by a divorced woman. In those days, a woman was expected to find life's purpose in homemaking or in menial work as secretary, waitress, housecleaner, stewardess, etc., regardless of her abilities and other interests.

Another difference we had from other households was that Mom was a vocal liberal and activist. Her recreational activities after work included becoming President of the school PTA, serving on the Rockville City Planning Commission, and being block chair for the Democratic Party (writing, mimeographing and distributing leaflets supporting Stevenson and Kennedy and Johnson).

Her political activities garnered her tickets to special events such as the Kennedy Inaugural Parade in January 1961. We traveled by bus in a blizzard to get to that event. I remember that we were given "Kennedy periscopes" so that we could watch his motorcade as it drove by us on that snowy afternoon and evening. We finally got home at 12:30 am and it was a very long day, trudging in the snow. Mom took Linda to the Democratic Convention when Kennedy was nominated and also gave her tickets to one of the five Lyndon Johnson Inaugural Balls.

Maryland has quite a political history. When I lived there, at least half of Marylanders embraced Southern politics, often mused that the wrong side had won in the Civil War and considered themselves Southerners. Many of the other half of the citizenry called themselves moderates. And then there we were, a tiny minority of self-proclaimed progressives. Among the latter were my Mom, maybe Linda, and me. We knew that our politics made us stick out. In our society at that time, the concept of freedom of speech was valued. So, just as we felt that others were entitled to their points of view, we perceived that others supported our rights to our points of view. No hate was generated by political perspective in that day and at that time. The whole country was transitioning away from the ravings of the Joseph McCarthy period into the dynamic 1960s, from fear mongering to love thy neighbor and peace. A big change.

We supported integration of our neighborhood. When the first black family moved into Twinbrook during the late 1950s, we welcomed them, included them in many activities and established long-lasting friendships. We walked with the family's children to the school bus and socialized with them. We encouraged them to have their friends visit the neighborhood and looked forward to the day when our neighborhood could be enriched by diversity among neighbors.

The first racial integration in Montgomery County happened when I was in junior high school. Rockville was one of the first cities in Montgomery County and in Maryland to bus children to schools and to end school segregation. By the time I was in high school, my classes were totally integrated. Friends who grew up in neighboring cities have told me Richard Montgomery High School was closely watched for its success or failure with integration because it was the first high school to be fully integrated. Although integrated, strong prejudice was all too obvious. Many students chose not to have anything to do with members of a different racial group or religion.

My high school friends and I devoted ourselves to integrating local enterprises, including Glen Echo Park, the local amusement park which had a "whites only" policy since its opening. With a group called "Students Against Discrimination" we picketed and marched for freedom and for integration.

My Mom hosted many families coming to DC from Alabama (Birmingham and Selma) when they marched to protest segregation. In the early 1960s, these folks stayed at our house often. We also hosted guests from other countries who were traveling around the U.S., connecting through an exchange arranged through our cooperative grocery store, through my mother's job, or just by word of mouth.

Mom was curious about the world and continued to be thirsty for new ideas and experiences throughout her life. She made our home stimulating. Nana made it comfortable.

The only unhappiness I remember growing up was my middle sister bullying me terribly.

I remember the time she held my head down in the deep water of the community swimming pool—it seemed like for hours. In another big fight, she hit me with her bullwhip! I fought back with an old broken umbrella. She had a very cruel streak. She was the bully of the house and I was the baby of the family (or as she always put it "the cry baby of the house") and her target. She and I shared a bedroom until the bullwhip incident. Shortly after that, Mom gave up her own bedroom. Ellen got Mom's bedroom and Mom got a bed in the bedroom I had shared with Ellen.

When I was in high school, I hung out a lot with one of my best friends, Beverly, who was black. Another friend, Ann, invited our whole group of friends to a slumber party at her house. Then Ann retracted Beverly's invitation, stating that her mother had said that she couldn't have a black friend spend the night. We all canceled out of the party because we couldn't tolerate that kind of prejudice. Rockville had its share of religious and racial bigotry and it divided the entire community.

My oldest sister, Linda, and I have always been very close. We look alike, walk alike, and love each other a lot. After she got her driver's license, we used to go out to dinner at the local Hot Shoppe's to eat. (It was akin to the local Denny's.) My grandmother would routinely cook with her nose running and a Kleenex up her sleeve. We suspected (or possibly knew) that Nana was dripping into the food she cooked. So, Linda and I would head out to eat so we wouldn't have to eat at home. The hardest part was not laughing explosively when we sat around the evening meal. She is my best friend, has protected me from tough situations over the years, and has helped me get through hard times. We formed a tight bond from early in our lives. We look like our father – dark hair and eyes, and tall – we don't match with our blonde mother or blonde middle sister. My middle sister was sexy and unlike us in many ways. My mother had to spend extra energy trying to keep up with her. She left the public high school after 10th grade and was sent to an exclusive private high school in Washington, DC. Later, she went to two years of college, and got married. Of the three of us, my middle sister turned out to be the most "traditional." We have very few things in common.

When I was 15, my mother called a house meeting. She wanted us to make a house decision about whether to get a new car or go to Europe for a month. The proposed European trip involved travelling by train on Eurail passes, and visiting any countries we wanted to see. I voted for a new car, but fortunately, my mom and sisters had better sense and voted to go to Europe. We had an astonishing time, and traveled to Paris,

Barcelona, Nice, Florence, Rome, Lucerne, Amsterdam, London (by ferry, sitting in the bar, and singing along with old English and Irish pub songs), Dublin and all around Ireland. At that time, I fully acknowledged and accepted my travel addiction – which I have to this day.

In 1963, Martin Luther King made his famous speech, "I Have a Dream," and led the March on Washington. Unbelievably, I took a babysitting job that day so that some adult friends of my family could go to the march. I'll never stop regretting it. Of course, my mother and almost everyone else I knew went.

I remember the exact day that John Kennedy was shot. I came home from school and heard it on the news. It was incomprehensible. We all sat and sobbed for hours. We had placed great hope in Kennedy's presidency.

Another one of my best friends was Bobby Israel. We met in school and he would sometimes drive me home after school. He was black. My mother worried about retaliation if I were seen in a car he was driving. It was ok when we went to a group meeting or to a protest with a car full of kids. Mom told me that she was worried and I was surprised that she would say anything like that. I didn't take her advice, but it was the only time I can think of that she allowed community opinion to make her fearful enough to advise me to be careful. I hate prejudice and I refuse to back down when I see it. We had quite an argument about that.

I graduated from Richard Montgomery High School in 1965. I was very social and politically active in high school and not especially studious. My grades reflected this—I was a C+/B- student—not bad considering I didn't study. I was most interested in politics and political action. In junior high and high school, I always had a diverse group of friends, black and white. Several of my conservative teachers were offended by my politics and activism over the years, but I spent no time worrying about that. I had a steady boyfriend, Ricky, for the last two years of high school, and I was active in school musicals and extracurricular political events and subjects outside of school. There were drugs available in my high school, but I didn't know about it at the time. Later, my high school boyfriend told me he had smoked pot in high school which came as a total surprise to me.

When I was about to graduate from high school, Sharyn Duffin, a dear friend and fellow activist, contracted spinal meningitis. She got inadequate medical care from the beginning of her illness. In my opinion, this was because she was black. The local segregated hospital made no effort to diagnose or treat her, leading her to become permanently disabled. Even though she went on to graduate from Antioch College with spectacular grades, she has had a tough life. Her mother, Norma, remained a good friend of my mother's throughout my mother's life. I kept in contact with Sharyn through my mother at first, then through ham radio transmissions, letters and finally email. Our friendship has been important to me through the years. I was able to meet up with Sharyn at my 40th high school reunion a few years ago.

When it was time for me to look around for colleges-I had two fundamental concerns. What should I major in and where should I go? My mother had some guests come over for dinner. The man was E.G. Marshall, who was an actor on The Defenders, a television show about lawyers. His daughter came along. She was beautiful, smart and funny. And she had been a philosophy major in college. Talking with her convinced me to make philosophy my college major. Prior to that, I actually hadn't been drawn to any specific field. Unlike my son, who has been passionate about studying World War II and history since he was in fifth grade, I did not have an academic passion. I did know that I wanted to go to a college, which was very far away from Twinbrook.

I was happy to leave Rockville, and Maryland. I was tired of having to fight for civil rights in every situation, tired of facing prejudice whenever I went out with my friends. I was angry that racist jokes were so prevalent. I didn't understand why the Bill of Rights was being trampled upon so openly. I did want to be living in a part of the country where prejudice was less formidable. I was ready to leave Maryland even though I had found comfort, companionship and even inspiration while living there. However, I was impatient with the slow progress being made to integrate our society, especially in a state that liked to identify itself with the southern perspective, as Maryland did.

After seeing and fighting the prejudice in Maryland, I wanted to head north. I applied at colleges far away from home. About 95% of my high school's graduates always went to the local teachers' colleges – Towson State or Frostburg—but I knew I didn't want to go there. One of the places I applied to was the University of Bridgeport in Connecticut. I was accepted there, and started in the fall of 1965 as a philosophy major.

Of the 8,000 students, half were commuters from the Bridgeport area. It was about forty-five minutes from New York, and many students went to New York to drink because the drinking age was eighteen. I did like to go to Greenwich Village, and a bar "The Irish Pub." But mostly, I only went to New York to protest the war in Vietnam.

Almost as soon as my mother and grandmother dropped me off at college, they sold our suburban house in Rockville, and moved into the northwest section of Washington, D.C. My mother was even more glad to leave Rockville than I was. As a single parent, she had worked very hard to give us a secure and comfortable childhood. Now, as an empty nester, she was ready to pursue the life she had put on hold. She loved living in DC and lived near Dupont Circle, in the Adams Morgan part of town. It was and is a great mix of people, restaurants, languages, smells and influences. It was perfect for her. My grandmother went along on the move, too. My mother went back to school and got her teaching credential, and then her Masters' Degree, in Reading Instruction. She could finally work at the job she wanted after all those years seeking job security as a single parent raising three daughters. She taught in inner city Washington and loved it, although was very hard for her. She was a quiet, thoughtful and determined teacher. She had a hard time with classroom management with the DC kids. I remember that she would get severe laryngitis for the first couple of weeks of every semester. She found the teaching experience most rewarding when she specialized in reading strategies and comprehension, working with much smaller groups of kids. She took great delight in meeting former students on the street or on buses. She also taught adults how to read and write at a local Senior Center and worked on an oral history project writing about their lives. She was always busy.

I was supposed to be ready to embark on adulthood. I turned eighteen soon after I began college. The next 25 years would be hazardous, to say the least. I had to survive drugs, a divorce, and a life after a divorce, Peoples Temple and Jonestown, a carjacking, the AIDS epidemic, Synanon, parenting, and along the way, trauma and the death of my naiveté. The only-slightly-crooked lifeline on my palm vastly understates the road I traveled. I had been treading water in high school. I was ready to dive into my life.

My Senior Picture, Richard Montgomery High School 1965

Caption: My friends and I leaving for the Senior Prom, 1965

CHAPTER 3
College Days

While I was at home in high school, I was the perfect daughter. I didn't drink or try any drugs. The only time I even smoked cigarettes was when I had a slumber party and a bunch of my girlfriends and I tried a few. It was so disgusting we didn't even want to play at that. I was determined not to get pregnant in high school, so was a virgin (just barely) when I entered college. I had been a good rule-follower at home. When I went to college, I actually wanted to get to know who I was – what I liked and didn't and what I wanted. One commonly dispensed prescription had wide-ranging impact. Birth control pills had just been introduced to the general public and that affected the whole generation, and certainly freed me up from the fear of pregnancy at a young age.

I was enthusiastic in general and loved college. I roomed with a girl from New York who had her next fifteen years all mapped out. Her plan was to graduate from college, get married to her football-playing fiancé, attend graduate school, and have two children. I didn't have much in common with her. My life was more free-floating (and interesting). I lived on campus all three years that I attended but lived in apartments off campus and worked during the summers. My first college boyfriend, Charles, was the Chancellor of some fraternity. After attending several fraternity parties, and cleaning vomit out of the girls' bathrooms at the end of the evenings, I decided I wasn't destined to be a drinker. I already knew I wasn't the sorority type. Fairly soon, I found out I wasn't his type either.

My next boyfriend was Turkish; and his nickname was "Altan." He was a political science major and taught me a lot about Turkish culture. He didn't agree with my view of American politics and was very conservative in his view of public displays of affection, or opposition to the government. I was more of a free spirit. He continually told me that I couldn't possibly be a virgin because I was definitely too friendly. He thought that he could tell that about me. He was wrong about that, too. My mother advised me against getting too serious with him because Turkish culture would radically inhibit me. She and I didn't have to worry. Since his parents wouldn't have allowed him to ever marry me, and since he would never do anything that would alienate them, we broke up when he graduated. He did call my mother a few years later, checking up on me. By then I was in California.

Beginning in 1963 and up until 1970, the world—and specifically my world—was in turmoil. I was finishing up my high school years and jumping into college during those formative years. The war in Vietnam continued. John Kennedy, Bobby Kennedy, Martin Luther King and Malcolm X were all killed. And though some inroads were being made against pervasive prejudice, they were too little, too late. I was frustrated by the world around me, even though I was in the protected space called college. I marched, got tear-gassed, wrote letters, called elected officials, and marched some more. I was very active in trying to better the world. I was president of the campus Student League for Human Rights for a couple of years. We toyed with the idea of becoming a branch of the Students for a Democratic Society, to join the national movement. We decided to maintain our independence from them, while participating in the national protests, teach-ins, and activities. This turmoil over the war and the wave of assassinations from the 1960s politicized many of the youth.

Socially, I had a lot of friends. I was bored by the sorority sisters and those who had planned out their whole lives. The friends I spent the most time with were an eclectic bunch. Two of the girls were biker-types who were also English majors, who used drugs frequently and who had exquisitely creative and exotic minds. Judy was the one most different from me, but we formed a friendship and shared housing over the summers. Now I wonder if they were stoned most of the time – but I have never been good at reading the clues when people around me were high. I am glad that I didn't get too involved in drinking or drugs. I saw firsthand how my mother and father drank on a daily basis and smoked.

In college, I also participated in a group called Honest to God. It was a discussion group to determine if God existed – and if not, how do you explain life? I did try to figure it all out, but at some point, I lost interest in the issue and dropped out of that group. Eventually, I just decided that with the inequalities in the world, there couldn't be a "just" god.

I had just come home to Washington, for spring break in 1968 when Martin Luther King was shot. My friends were coming down to Washington, D.C. to have Easter break with me. The moment we arrived at my mother's apartment, there was a curfew on the street. Some of my visiting friends were still in transit and were gathered up and put in the Washington Armory, a sports arena, and held until the next day to keep them off the street. No amount of explaining could get them released. My mother's apartment overlooked the Washington Hilton, at the corner of Connecticut Avenue and Columbia Road, NW. We watched the army take over the underground parking area of the Hilton, and saw army tanks go up and down the streets, patrolling all night. We had to be careful looking out the windows so we wouldn't be mistaken as snipers. It was a traumatic and tense time for America, and for us. In the late 1960s, civil liberties were trounced on but Martin Luther King had always been a voice of sanity and compassion. I remember feeling powerless.

My university campus was politically conservative then, and I continued on my unremarkable academic journey for three years. In my junior year, my work scholarship included tutoring and teaching arts and crafts at a local housing project within walking distance of the campus. I went into the project and taught, and then I would walk back to my Symbolic Logic class – a requirement for Philosophy and Math majors. My classes were totally irrelevant, besides being hard. I lost interest in the theoretical discussion of philosophy, and flunked out after my junior year. My counselor told me that I was the first student he'd met to flunk out that late in a college career. That's me – one of a kind. I had lost the vision of why I needed college. I loved working in the nearby housing project. The study of philosophy didn't engage my heart. I was idealistic then and felt the work in the project had grabbed me. Also I was very active in opposing the Vietnam War and I was self-educating by being involved in activities that enriched my life.

One time, when we were in a huge march in New York City, Judy brought her little dog. We had been walking, and carrying a cup of water for the dog since it was a hot day. All of a sudden, the police shot tear gas canisters all over and around us. I remember we got a napkin and put it in the water and held it over the dog's mouth and nose. It was quite scary for all of us, and we were especially angry that we had been marching peacefully, to demonstrate our freedom of speech, and trying to voice our opposition to the unjust Vietnam War, and we got tear-gassed. It was devastating. The abandonment of civil rights during that time was alienating us from the larger culture.

After leaving college, I started working at the Connecticut Welfare Department as a Medicaid Intake worker, and I took college courses at night. On my job, I took applications of people applying for Medicaid. I spoke some social Spanish, but increased my knowledge of Spanish to include every ache, pain, break, and illness imaginable. I loved it.

From my sophomore year until the end of my junior year of college, I was dating another "revolutionary," Robert. We protested together, marched on the Pentagon, got tear-gassed together, and grew our hair long together. He read James Joyce and since James Joyce was my mother's favorite author, I rather thought my mother would love him. I was wrong. She may have taken offense to him smoking weed in the front living room of her apartment. In any case, I was in love with him, so we dated a few years and then decided to get married. My sister Linda had come for a visit from California and we decided to get married while she was visiting. In January 1969, a Justice of the Peace married us in a coastal park in Bridgeport. There was just a bit of snow on the ground. I wore my favorite tall brown boots. I was too unconventional for the all-white bridal regalia. Robert's family wasn't too enthusiastic about the location, but it was my wedding. They'd had their own chance to orchestrate their weddings. My adjustable peace-symbol wedding ring wasn't too popular with them either.

After we got married, I continued working at the welfare department, and my husband studied engineering. I was supporting him as he was finishing his fourth and final year of electrical engineering. In the final semester, he changed majors to become an architect, which meant he signed on for a few more years of school. He worked part-time at the local discount store, while I worked full-time. His parents were very kind, conservative folks and hadn't let us live together until we were married. On Sundays, we all went as a family to the nearby Town and Country Diner. I definitely wonder now how long that would have gone on. I just know that I would have been miserable in that environment and can hardly believe I did it then. But at that time, we were a happily married, employed, and model couple living near some family members, sort of waiting to develop a family or do whatever other young couples were doing. We were happily married for about nine months.

That was when Judy called me from New York, asking for help. Her boyfriend was addicted to drugs, and she had to relocate so she could stop using. I invited her to come back to Bridgeport, move into our apartment building, and try to get her life together. She came. She was enormously creative and brilliant as always. She also had a different slant on life and friendship than I did. She would come over in the evening and hang out with us. Both she and Robert liked whiskey. I tried most stuff that came my way, but I just didn't like drinking. Often I would just go off and go to sleep, leaving these trusted friends to get drunk. That wasn't a good plan. Soon after she returned to Bridgeport, she and Robert started their relationship. Robert said that he was separating from me, to be with her. He moved back home to mama. She moved back to New York. We arranged for him to have the van on weekends, so she could come up and they would stay overnight in the van. In that affair, I lost both of my best friends. I went through a very low period in terms of my self-esteem and wasn't sure what I had done wrong for this "life-long commitment" to end so abysmally. I was much like other married or committed individuals who find their relationships unexpectedly falling apart.

Bill was one of my first boyfriends after my separation from my husband. He was going through a divorce at the same time. Immediately after Robert and I separated, I made a series of particularly lousy choices. Bill was the beginning move of my cycle down. Once, we went to the local seaside park and made love. On the way back to my apartment, he told me that he had had sex with six women under that tree, that same day. I hadn't thought of him as any kind of permanent boyfriend but I did think his sexual exploits were bizarre. Another time, he came over and gave me a big black pill. He said that it would make me really mellow. After a few minutes, he said he was going out and that I'd be fine. When I told him I had just put the pill away, he just couldn't believe that I hadn't taken it. I think he called it a Black Beauty. He was hoping I wouldn't even miss him while he went to another tryst, I guessed.

The highlight of going out with him, though, was that we went to Woodstock together. We went to visit some of his friends out in the countryside in upstate New York, fairly near Woodstock. I used LSD there, one of the few times I ever took it. I can remember being on acid, and sitting on the farmhouse roof. I don't know how I got up there, but I remember sitting and feeling my butt burning on the hot tiles. I somehow did jump down. Later, when I was straight, I couldn't fathom how I got up or how I got down without breaking my neck. After a while, a group of us went out to Woodstock. We drove in as close as we could, and then walked a long, hot, dusty, and hilly road into the arena area. It was awesome, surrounded by a hundred thousand gyrating bodies. Just like you see the steam come up from the road on a hot day, people seemed to be springing up from the ground all around. There were adults and young children, naked and clothed, and pets. There were loudspeakers but unfortunately the music was almost inaudible and with the best musicians of the time! I loved all parts of it except the smell. The smell stays with me even until this day. There was never anything like it. The hard-packed red soil was unforgiving and trampled down. Nothing was absorbed into the soil. The toilets were overflowing and no longer usable. There were ponds where people were dancing, but they were clogged and drying up fast, adding to the pollution of the whole area. You could buy any drugs you wanted. People walked through the crowds saying, "Acid? Speed? Coke? Hash? Pot? The BEST you ever tried!" But most of the folks who came didn't have any money left, and had brought their own stashes anyway. My high school boyfriend had come with his brother, who did buy the acid. He ended up in an institution for his adult life, since it scrambled his brain waves permanently.

There has never been a close copy of the ambiance or dynamism of Woodstock. It just can't be replicated. It truly did feel that we were all of one mind. I was delighted that I had been there and seen it, at least part of the time straight. After we left, we returned to the farm and then went back to Bridgeport, where I was still living. We stopped seeing each other shortly after that.

The Black Panthers started a free breakfast program in the recreation center right next to the welfare department's building in the project. I started volunteering every morning to serve breakfast. I wasn't allowed to cook or touch any of the food because I was white, and the point being made was that blacks were helping blacks and Hispanics-and that they would do the actual cooking and serving so that kids could see it. But I could clean tables and hand out the plates, napkins, and silverware. It was reverse racism, but I felt useful and proud that I was helping in an effort that I thought was great, giving a good breakfast to poor kids living in that same project. I firmly believe that kids learn by adults and others modeling important actions. It was very important for these kids to see who was taking care of them. I felt like my being there was a statement, too. We all have to take care of the world's children. At these breakfasts, many kids were seeing things they were not seeing in their homes, in their communities, on television, or anywhere else in their lives. They could watch people, many of them men with their same skin color, nurturing them and feeding them wholesome food.

I started getting more involved with the Black Panthers, many of whom I had met at the Free Breakfasts and on my job. At one point, I had five Black Panthers living with me in my apartment for some months. Several would bring guns into my apartment, in guitar cases or in some other sort of disguise. I would attend meetings, as allowed. Once, there was a meeting in my kitchen. I was sat down and questioned about my ideas and political opinions. I guess I passed, because the business meeting went on. Their meetings were mostly teaching from Panther pamphlets and books. They organized their protests also.

On one occasion, some of us were sitting around in my apartment. My "boyfriend" E.C. was there, and another man either sat close to me, or pulled me to sit on his lap. Someone fired a gun, and it hit the leg of the guy flirting with me. The men rushed him out to the hospital, where he reported that he was shot through his open window. I stayed to clean up the blood spattered on the floor of my apartment and the hallways. It was not a unique event. I was almost raped, my friend's car was stolen and stripped, and more. One conversation I recall was E.C. telling me I could earn money for sex from his friends and acquaintances. I asked him why I would do that for money. I didn't need the money, because I had a good job. He told me I wouldn't be getting the money anyway. He would. With everyone hanging out in my apartment, there were times when people would use drugs there, too. But, generally, the Black Panthers knew, as I did, that you could not mix activism with drug use – you were easy prey for the police.

In late January 1970, I met up with a former college date, Richard. We went out a few times. Later the same week, he called me to say he had caught a Sexually Transmitted Disease from me. I had been asymptomatic so went to my doctor. I ended up in the hospital for several days.

I believe that one of the consequences of this STD was that the infection caused scar tissue, which blocked my tubes so that I couldn't get pregnant, at least without serious medical assistance. I feel fortunate that I did not try to parent a child through the following ten years or so. I don't know if I could have survived those years if I had been a parent. If nothing else got me first, my guilt would have crushed me. So, fortunately for all concerned, I didn't birth a child during that extremely rocky time. Even though I was in the hospital, E.C. and other roommates didn't bother coming to see me, but friends of theirs did ransack my apartment and strip a car I had borrowed from a friend. Linda invited me (insisted, in fact) to move to San Francisco with her. I was finally ready for that.

I actually can't figure out why it was such a struggle for me to regroup and get back on track after my separation. I had the perfect mother who was hardworking, attentive, and dedicated to important causes. Even without a father in the home I came from a very stable life. Living in the same house for all of your elementary and high school years is almost unheard of these days. But I hadn't found what I was looking for and couldn't stop searching. So, still reeling and still searching, I moved out to California to live with Linda.

I remember one significant personal breakthrough Linda and I had when we were sitting atop a famous hotel in San Francisco, having cocktails. We whined about my mother's parenting style, and her shortcomings. We sort of looked at each other and said, almost in unison, "Well, I guess it is up to us now. We're adults." That rang true to me even if it was more than I could handle for a while. We charged ahead with our lives. Unfortunately for me, I was rather like Don Quixote.

There was a part of me that was very self-destructive. As soon as I hit town, I was right in the middle of a mess. Linda bought a car, and I dated the car salesman. I would have never bought a car from him. He was no better and no worse than others I had dated earlier. But, he was hooked up with a nurse who was herself a junkie, and who supplied him with drugs as well. Even to this day, I can't understand the part of me so willing to disengage my brain and go blindly into harm's way. For a time in college, I tied it to political action, knowing that my stance was unpopular with the local police and the politicos. But, the magnetism drawing me to danger is deeply rooted in my psyche. Somehow, I always "just" escaped the abyss. There were other sordid misadventures during my first few months in San Francisco with an amateur porn filmmaker, and a cocaine-addicted ambulance-chasing attorney who tried to set up a threesome, to name a few. As each day passed, my life spun more and more out of control. I did it all, and barely survived.

I appeared to fit in with the hippie crowd in San Francisco, but that was not to be my path. The series of events that truly impacted my life began when Linda took me up to Redwood Valley, California, to meet Jim Jones and Peoples Temple. From there, my life went in a whole new direction.

CHAPTER 4
What is Peoples Temple?

When I walked into the Peoples Temple Church in Redwood Valley for the first time, I had long hair, lots of make-up, and a very short skirt. I was sort of a cross between a hippie and a streetwalker. My life was spiraling downwards.

In 1956, Pastor Jim Jones had started his ministry as "Wings of Deliverance." He soon changed the name to Peoples Temple. After visiting other churches, he had collected a group of stalwart supporters who believed in his message of equality and practical Christianity. By 1960, he and his wife Marceline had had one "homegrown" child, Stephan, and five adopted children including Agnes, Stephanie, Lew, Suzanne, and Jim Jr., children of all nationalities and colors. It was unusual in the early 1960s for a family or a church to be integrated. But he broke new ground.

In 1962, when the world was threatened by a possible nuclear holocaust, *Esquire* Magazine had written about the five safest places to live in the United States. Ukiah, California was listed as one of the five. In 1965, Jim brought about one hundred followers in rickety old cars from Indiana to Ukiah and the neighboring Redwood Valley. Several groups from Willits, a nearby community where Jim had first held services, got involved with Peoples Temple, including an Edgar Cayce study group and a commune with a Pentecostal background. Some of the most dedicated members joined up at this time including Garry Lambrev, Bonnie Beck, Carolyn Layton, Larry Layton, Karen

Tow, Carol Stahl, Neva Sly, and others. Another group of mostly black church members came up from San Francisco. There was a great divide at first because most of the new California members were progressive atheists, non-dogmatic Christians, Buddhists, or New Age types. Even the Baptists who joined from San Francisco were more progressive than the group that Jim had brought from the Midwest. But Jim soon brought us all together in one cohesive group, his core group of supporters. Later on, more traditional Christians joined in once the ministry started visiting San Francisco, Los Angeles, Seattle, and other smaller cities.

As soon as I entered the room in March 1970, I saw Jim Jones. He had black hair and a dark complexion, and was very striking. He generated a warmth and inclusion that bound everyone to him and to each other. He also had an enormous, enthusiastic church with a 300-member congregation full of people of all colors and ages. He had his own beautiful rainbow family and a collection of many other adults and children who were part of Peoples Temple and who were treated as his inner family. Some members were as strange as I was. He deftly navigated through all of the differences of religious views in each meeting. People listening for his religious and healing meetings heard that. His political and social statements were just what I had been searching for. He mentioned my heroes Angela Davis, Dennis Banks, Martin Luther King, Huey Newton, the Chicago Seven, and so many more. In his sermon, he caught my attention. I had been looking for a safe place to live and act on my convictions, but hadn't found a safe venue. I was losing my way. Unlike me, most of the people in the meetings were very conservative looking, in plain clothes, and brimming over with a pure, healthy glow. No one wore Sunday finery and jewels, but instead, everyone looked well scrubbed and down-to-earth. Here was an interracial church with an awesome choir singing about revolution, equality, freedom, and socialism. I could have listened to the choir for hours. The musicians were accomplished, and the singers poured out their hearts when they sang. The songs sounded as if they had been written by the individual singing. I learned later that many were old spirituals that had a few words changed. The melodies were hauntingly beautiful. Jim and everyone else talked about socialism and equality, and then lived it. I loved what I saw.

Still I didn't quite see myself fitting in there. I was into self-destruction. I don't know if I planned to come back later, after I hit an even lower bottom or not. I loved it there, and was glad it was there. I was just in a different place. Often I had smoked pot or hash the evening before. My whole life, I had heard my mother's tirades against the hypocrisy in churches and hypocrisy in general. I didn't want to use drugs on Saturday and then go listen in a church, looking pious and pure. So I was ready to stop going. I chose to continue with my San Francisco lifestyle. Then Linda told me of another woman, Liz, who was into astrology, Tarot cards, and the occult. She was planning to go up and evaluate and even challenge Jim. I wasn't usually busy on Sunday mornings, so we went up another time. This time, Liz and I became enamored with the whole effort. Liz admired Jim because he was a Native American, a Marxist, and a healer. Even though there was no formal pledge to sign, we each acknowledged that we had decided to become part of it. She has a somewhat different recollection of these weeks, but this is how I remember them. From the minute I walked into the Temple, people of all ages and races befriended me. My own discomfort in the way I was dressed or looked was not mirrored in those who came around me. They were genuinely kind. As I looked around, others in the building seemed to be comfortable, happy and engaged also. The Temple services were never just fashion shows and places to wear your newest duds. They had accepted me as one of them and I had eventually accepted that I was in a place I belonged. And Liz had not been able to challenge Jim. She was enthralled by what she had seen with his "gift" as it was called.

The Sunday services had a set routine. First, the magnificent interracial and intergenerational choir would sing the most exhilarating hymns and songs. Many of the songs were original, and many were re-written to reflect the Temple philosophy. Jim's wife Marcie often sang "Black Baby," about Jimmy, their adopted black child. Jim and Marcie had been the first white couple to adopt a black baby in the state of Indiana. An ex-convict named Melvin Johnson would sing "Walk a Mile in My Shoes." Everyone who sang seemed to be singing about himself or herself, but we each saw ourselves in the songs too. The music would unify all of us, and the enthusiasm would have everyone up and dancing. Then Jim would come to the pulpit. Sometimes he wore a crimson robe or he would wear this worn-looking red-striped velour shirt. He would preach and teach and reflect on the current sorry state of the country. Everyone would get the message they wanted to hear. I was interested in the politics and never bothered about the Christian theology or Bible admonitions. Others wanted the Bible discussed and preached and they heard that. Jim was well versed in the Bible and could spin a story with biblical quotes easily. Then he would turn it into a socialist or idealist message. He would draw parallels between then and now, or Job and someone he knew facing hardship now. He was a thespian of the highest order, and yet preached to a universal level. To say Jim was a wordsmith totally understates his genius. He was "all things to all people" in his sermons. He presented something for everyone.

I loved listening to his messages. They challenged me and taught me a lot about current events in the world and in politics. I hated to miss any part of his political sermons. The religious sermons in the more public meetings were less engaging for me, so I never felt bad for missing them. I felt that the political message was where his heart was, as was mine, and that the religious sermons were something he tolerated in order to politicize and even re-educate people who came solely for the religious message.

He would have a "healing" time after the sermon. Over the years, many people joined the Temple so that their loved ones or they would be cured of an illness or protected from another sort of evil. Jim was seen as a protector, and a lot of people felt themselves to be in danger of illness or violence. First we would hold hands and sit quietly for a moment. Usually, he would put on his dark sunglasses. In Redwood Valley in 1970, he only wore them during that one part.

I do believe that Jim had a gift of clairvoyance or ultra-sensitivity to those in the meeting. It is difficult to find a name for this ability. I have never seen anything like it. Since people do acknowledge extra-sensory perception, I believe that Jim had some altered state of understanding that he used during this time. In any case, at this time of Meeting, Jim would call out a name of a person in attendance, and tell that person something personal. He would tell them that they had just seen a doctor on Friday and had been given some bad news, or they had a call that morning from a sick aunt in Texas, or they had a painful headache. Sometimes, he would call out a place and ask who had been to the

Farmers' Market on Friday afternoon in Hunter's Point, or who had been driving a red car and had a near head-on collision somewhere on Saturday at seven a.m. He would identify the person and have the person stand up. Then he would hold his hands out or jump off the stage to go and hold hands. Sometimes he would have the congregation singing softly, and sometimes it would be quiet.

I had heard some references to "healing" in my life but had dismissed it as impossible and fantasy. I was more than cynical that such a thing existed. Then, near where I was sitting, or near where friends were sitting, we saw people pass bloody masses of cancer. If I hadn't seen it up close with my own eyes, there is no way I would have believed it. But I did see it often enough to become convinced that there is such a thing. I have since found out that some of these "healings" were staged but I have no way of knowing how many. At that time, I thought they were all real, and still believe that many were real because for years afterward, many of those same people who had been healed enthusiastically confirmed it in conversations with me. One specific time, he called out a member named Bonnie who had a good friend, Don, in the Peace Corps in South America. Jim told her that Don had been in a different country than his assignment and that he was having a hard time with something. Bonnie thought that it wasn't true because she knew where Don was supposed to be. She found out later that Jim had been exactly right. Often Jim would have information about very obscure facts that were later verified.

Jim used the healings as a way to get more members into Peoples Temple. Once there, he would work at re-directing them into activism. He wanted a heaven on earth. He asked people to ponder why they thought they should wait until they were dead to have heaven. The healings could be a few minutes or an hour, depending on Jim. Once, when I first started coming around, Jim told me that I should stay close to the Temple. He said that I could look on my back door, where I was living in San Francisco with Linda, and see the words, "We are living hear," or something like that. I remember finding the words and "hear" was misspelled. I was never that charmed by those kinds of messages. I was so very impressed with the political message and the huge family Jim had drawn together, I don't think anything else mattered to me.

After the healing part of the service, everyone would hug, eat a communal meal, and socialize. Jim would walk around the congregation and check in with everyone. He would walk around the grounds and just take it all in. He was easily approachable and exuded calmness and concern. Kids would go run outside, swim, or play with the animals. In the Redwood Valley Temple, there was a lovely pool at the back of the church. I loved that there was a pool where Jim baptized folks, but also where kids would go swimming in the summer right in the church. That was the Sunday, Redwood Valley schedule before we started our travels.

The grounds of the Redwood Valley Temple complex held several residences besides Jim's and covered a couple of acres. It was on East Road, one of the two main roads in Redwood Valley. There were many dogs, cats, and other animals, living on the property, too. One dog, a purebred German shepherd, had atrophied hind legs. One of the inventive members up in Redwood Valley, Walter Cartmell, built a set of rollers that could be strapped on the dog to allow him to walk all around the blacktop area and back to Jim's house. Walter was part of the original South Indiana church group that followed Jim to California, and he and his family lived on the church property. Many members were people with great ingenuity and skills. I thought it was great that Jim lived right at the back of the blacktop parking area, right next to the church building. As I met and got to know to know Jim's wife Marceline and his great family, I was even more comfortable being there. Marceline was a kind and thoughtful person. She was an inspector of nursing homes for the State of California and had no hesitation about exposing and remedying substandard care for seniors. She was a crusader in her area of health care.

During my eighth time visiting in Redwood Valley, I met up with another charismatic and hilarious fellow, Chris Lewis. He had just joined at the end of 1969, after he got out of prison. He had kicked the heroin habit after joining the Temple. I even remember he was wearing a yellow flowered shirt. Yellow is my favorite color and I thought that was a sign of sorts. He was so handsome in it. We spent time at the meetings in Redwood Valley and then dated regularly in San Francisco, where he also lived. I thought I had found my match and I couldn't believe my good fortune. Here, I could be in an interracial relationship with a handsome, sexy, funny, and wild guy, and with Jim there to protect me, kind of like a father. Jim even seemed a bit like my father, dark hair, a ruddy complexion, always smooth. People did call him Father.

I also got to know many of those in Chris' inner circle. One of my best friends was Alice Ingram. She was a good friend of Chris' aunt, Verdella. Alice and her daughter, Ava, moved up to Redwood Valley and opened a care home for disabled girls. Her husband Jimmy kept his good job in San Francisco and commuted up whenever he could. They were happy to be out of the city and raising their daughter around friends in Redwood Valley. Jimmy's sister, Vera, joined the Temple until she went off to college. She and her husband John were one of the first interracial couples to join in Redwood Valley. They all felt like they were part of my extended family, and it was just amazing having such a vibrant, mixed, extended family.

Chris was one of the members who preferred to remain at an arm's distance from Jim. He was in awe of Jim, and appreciated how Jim had helped him get off of drugs and had provided him with legal counsel and support. That allowed Chris to get a suspended sentence instead of returning to prison. Chris gave Jim all the credit for saving his life and was happy to be on call and to help wherever he was needed, but still had his own life to live in San Francisco. Shortly after we started dating, we moved in together. We lived in a room above his Aunt Verdella's house in San Francisco for about five months. I had Chris and I had his family, whom I loved. When I said that Chris had "cleaned up" after joining Peoples Temple that was mostly true. I admit I wasn't that determined to keep on the "straight and narrow" myself. And we lived 120 miles from Jim. Still, we survived, and made mostly good decisions. We smoked a little pot from time to time. Once, Chris came to Linda's job and sold boxes of new ceramic dishes, cheaply. They had "fallen off a truck," he said. He changed his behavior a lot to be a regular member, but still had his trick knee. Chris would have given his life for Jim, but would not give up his day-to-day activities.

At one point, we decided to move to Oakland where he had found a little cottage. We went to see it and spent one night there. There was no heat yet, so we left the oven on with the door open overnight. In the morning, the entire apartment was packed with cockroaches. We sprayed the whole place, left for a few days, and then came back. The cockroaches were so thick, you couldn't walk, and they nearly filled the toilet and all the surfaces. That time, it was easy to put my foot down and say no way. It is so strange that I could see that wasn't going to work, yet other horrific things didn't get me so alarmed or decisive.

In the late spring of 1970, we were in a Sunday night service in Redwood Valley. Jim called out my name in the meeting. I stood up. He looked directly at me and told me I should move up to Redwood Valley immediately. I loved the Temple, the philosophy, the political message and the whole atmosphere. I also liked being with Chris. Chris wasn't about to move to Redwood Valley, not right under Jim's nose. I immediately made plans to do what Jim said.

Moving up to Redwood Valley then was a very good decision for me. I was beginning to develop my own understanding of what was good for me. It was just a whisper, but I had some sense that remaining with Chris in the city was not a good arrangement for me. Jim told me to move and I agreed that it was about that time, so I moved.

Even though Jim told me to do it, I could have decided not to follow his advice. Some people have told me that being in Peoples Temple was a bad decision. There is no argument that it was a terrible decision for almost everyone who joined. Almost all of us perished. My feeling is that, looking at the decisions I had been making up to the day of joining Peoples Temple, it probably gave me the next seven years of my life. Left to my own devices, I might not have survived. It allowed me to outlive my own misadventures. And I felt I had a home there until the very end.

Jim, or someone, had arranged for me to move in with Jack Beam and his family, and into their small licensed family-care facility. I learned a lot there. I liked the family very much because they were such direct, hardworking and delightfully funny people. They included me in their lives right away, and it was a great match. In August of 1970, I left San Francisco and moved to Ukiah, the closest city to Redwood Valley, where many members lived and worked.

Most of the members had come with Jim from Indiana, and had been with him on trips out of the country and all around the US. Jack Beam and Archie Ijames were the Assistant Pastors and long-time members of Jim's congregations. Jack was one of a kind, as was his wife, Rheaviana. There are so many words that are meaningless out of context. After I met them, I truly knew the meaning of "salt of the earth." Jack and Rheaviana were so practical and so very articulate and funny that it was an education just being around them. I was delighted to get to eat Rheaviana's cooking. She introduced me to stale cornbread in milk with a little sugar, and some other delicious Midwestern foods with gravy. The Beam family had smart, dedicated members who helped me get more solidly on my own feet. I felt like a helium balloon then, and they had me tethered to their home. As with helium balloons, as the helium seeped out, the balloon sank back down to earth eventually. That was me. I settled in.

While living with the Beams, I got a job as a waitress and applied for other jobs. In the fall of 1970, I was hired to work at the Ukiah Welfare Department. I was an eligibility worker until March 1977.

From the moment I moved up to Redwood Valley, I loved it. I got more involved in Temple activities and felt like I had come home. The year I lived with the Beams was great because the whole family was entertaining, insightful, and warm. They welcomed me into their home with open arms. I learned a lot about the work ethic and the flow of endless work projects in the Temple from them.

By the end of 1971 the Temple had started traveling to have services along the west coast. We had one service a month in Seattle, one in Los Angeles and two in San Francisco. We started acquiring a fleet of used Greyhound buses, and we took enough enthusiastic and dedicated members to fill a building. We eventually eliminated Seattle as a regular monthly service and alternated between San Francisco and Los Angeles, and bought permanent Peoples Temple buildings in those two cities. We would go to San Francisco on Friday night, and then on to Los Angeles for services Saturday evening and Sunday morning. After the service, we would drive back, drop off members and a few buses at the Temple in San Francisco, and go back up to Redwood Valley with Jim's bus, number seven, and a few more.

Our services were drawing at least three hundred people in both San Francisco and Los Angeles. Some people would come to all of the meetings when Jim was in town. Others would come to one, and then go to their own church on Sunday. At that time, Jim was just spreading the word. People were drawn by word of mouth because there was no other church like us. In San Francisco, Glide Memorial Church was socially and politically active, but seemed to draw people with more money and more clothes to show off. Jim's role was to be socially and politically active, while making a point that church was not a fashion show. He preached that church was a place to put hands and feet on your prayers, and bring heaven now, not later.

We had thirteen buses in our fleet, and easily forty bus drivers. It was breathtaking driving a fleet of buses down the freeways at night. All of the drivers had ridiculous "handles" as we communicated to each other over our radios, and our banter was comical. I was an enthusiastic driver because it was so unbelievable to me that I would ever do something like that. Here I was, a philosophy major and drop out, driving a Greyhound-type bus all around California and then around the US. Sometimes the bus was full of members of all ages. On a few occasions, I drove Jim's bus.

Around this same time, we started doing some security around our church property and around Jim's house. Some in Redwood Valley were hostile to the integration we brought, and others didn't like the commotion of so many people and so much action in a rural community. It wasn't a harmonious time. We got some threats and we started being a little more careful about where we were and what was going on around us. Peoples Temple had moved into the area, looking like a new church. As our membership ballooned, each Temple building became an action center where we gathered regularly and where we developed more plans for expanding and becoming more involved. Jim and Peoples Temple had transformed into a huge ministry, yet we were in a tiny country town.

Outside of Jim's inner circle, there was no glass ceiling. We were expected to do our very best in all endeavors. No excuses were accepted. Jim often made the point that he never had a choice whether to do his job thoroughly and correctly, and he didn't give us that option either. It was tough love, but we accepted the challenge and frequently surprised ourselves. There was as much work and as much responsibility as anyone could handle. No stereotypes got in the way of all of us working hard and each job went to the person most gifted or trained in that area.

The flow of our regular meetings up and down California was similar. People would gather at the services. The choir would perform and individuals would sing soulful solos. They were outstanding. One of the Assistant Pastors, either Jack Beam or Archie Ijames at first, or

Johnny Brown from San Francisco, or Hue Fortson from Los Angeles, would get up and take a collection. Later on, Jim would come out with his sermon or talk. He'd speak for an hour or more. Then he would do a thorough collection for nearly an hour, passing the plates several times through the entire congregation. He would move into a healing service for another forty-five minutes and mix in some choir music. Finally, everyone would hug, and then join together for a big potluck meal. In San Francisco, the members had prepared home-cooked food, like greens, corn bread, chicken, cakes, and other scrumptious food for sale. All of the money they made would be donated to the church. That is much like other churches all across the country. In many ways, Peoples Temple could look like a mainstream church.

Early on, Jim invited some of the Chilean victims of torture to join us in meetings. We supported them while they tried to regain the independence of Chile. They had supported the elected president, Salvador Allende, before the United States government ousted him and installed General Augusto Pinochet. Allende had been killed. These Chileans told us some of their experiences at the hands of Pinochet's troops, horrific tortures. Since they spoke only Spanish, they told me and then I translated for Jim and the rest of the congregation. When Jim spoke, I'd translate what he had said back to them. That was a truly amazing job for me to do, over several months. They were brave people and they were driven to get justice, and to get the US out of their country's politics forever. They were as focused as we were. I was delighted that Jim had arranged for them to come and had taken them under his wing. Jim used their situation to educate all of us. It made me all the more devoted to the Temple.

When I arrived in San Francisco in March 1970, I had promptly filed for divorce from Robert, my ex-husband. In December of 1970, his fiancée Judy called me to ask when the divorce would be final. She had been my best friend until the two of them got together. She was anxious, since her marriage to Robert was planned for the next week. I wasn't that surprised that Robert hadn't called. I suppose that I hadn't expected him to have the character to call himself. But I was sorry to have to tell Judy that it would be final the next day. I also told her that I was getting married soon, too. I didn't actually want to continue to be seen as a victim. Even though my life had taken a whole new direction,

I hated that Robert and Judy had betrayed my trust. The only thing that did feel right was that I had closed the door on Bridgeport and I had found a place where I was at peace.

One of the little known facts about residents in the Temple was the regimen we went through. Jim would encourage us to do some healthy activities. Over the years, he encouraged us to sleep on our right sides so we wouldn't add extra pressure to our hearts or crush them. We took large doses of vitamin E, took fifty deep breaths in the morning to get our lungs clear, regularly had soybean products to guard against the effects of a nuclear war, took cold showers every day, and drank Dr. Pepper because of some medicinal value one of our doctors or nurses had read about. They told us that it stabilized our electrolytes. One member's cat was killed when it fell asleep inside a car's engine on a cold night, and the driver turned on the car the next morning. As a result, Jim asked us to knock on the hood before we got in any car. We would also walk around our cars three times before getting in, so that we could focus on the car and the driving, not on whatever hectic schedule we had been on. Once inside a car, we would sit and wait two minutes before starting our trip. That too was to get us to focus on a safe trip. The funniest part would be when we were coming home from work, or in some public non-Peoples Temple setting, and we would knock on our car hood and walk around the car three times, and then sit trance-like inside. I'm sure that just confirmed to everyone that we were crazy. But it was one of our ceremonies and we all did it; it unified us that we were all practicing that same ritual.

Amazingly, with all of our travel around the state and the country, we had only one person die in a traffic accident. Dorothy Worley fell asleep behind the wheel while driving home to Redwood Valley from a Planning Commission meeting in San Francisco. The buses never had an accident. You could call that miraculous, or at the very least, astounding.

An unwritten but often expressed and very important rule was that every car going to any destination must have the front seats integrated. We always traveled in integrated groups and we needed to reflect our own values. In many settings, people sit according to the groups they are the most comfortable with – teachers with teachers, doctors with doctors, and sports team members with fellow members because that is easy. Jim insisted from day one that we acknowledge that pattern and change it. We didn't sit with our housemates, or with folks who lived in the same city or with people doing the same jobs outside of or inside Peoples Temple, nor with people the same color as ourselves. We met and knew each other in Peoples Temple because of his insistence. We became a family because we worked at it. We were re-educated and our children never had to un-learn those same lessons because they learned about equality every day in every setting.

In some ways, Jim was the kind of parent each of us would want to be or have. Each time he would introduce us to a new ritual or routine, he would explain it fully. He would present it as if it made perfect sense to do it. Just the kookiness of it was enough for us to find it entertaining. We were internalizing the notion that things had to make sense only to us – not neighbors, not acquaintances, no one else. The rebelliousness in each of us allowed us to practice these actions. These rituals bonded us together even more.

We were very busy. The Beams had a family care home, so I helped them a bit there. ("A bit" being an overstatement since Rheaviana and the rest were like whirlwinds passing through when they were cleaning, cooking, and maintaining the home!) I kept busy, too. I worked at the welfare department fulltime, and had numerous other obligations.

I have thought about whether I was more receptive to Jim because I came from a "broken home." I don't actually know. In some ways, Jim did look like my father. However, there were many people in Peoples Temple, with all kinds of fathers from the best to the worst. I think that if I had been raised by my father or both of my parents, and had been as idealistic and naïve as I was in 1970, I would still have been drawn to the family Jim created in Peoples Temple. This family had people of all races, all economic levels, all interests and diverse talents. The group of Peoples Temple members was just so rich, vibrant, and dedicated. I don't know if I would have been better able to look ahead to where Jim might end up taking us. I just don't know. I can't find a common thread in the backgrounds of those of us who went to Peoples Temple and felt at home.

In the early 1970s, many young people joined Peoples Temple. We lived in various communes. Each commune was self-governed. We shared all the chores, which left time to get a lot of work done outside the house. Of course, we spent no time on recreation!

I moved out of the Beams' care home and into various communes that we started around Calpella and Redwood Valley. First, I lived at the Eastside Calpella commune, across the street from Temple members Tim and Grace Stoen and next door to Vicki Moore and her family. She was Archie Ijames' daughter. About eight of us lived there. Eastside Calpella House had a three-bedroom house in the front and another big dorm in back, connected by the laundry room. We established our communal etiquette there and then spread it around to other communes. We learned to share our chores evenly and maintain a simple home for ourselves, and it was extremely gratifying. Most of the people living there were the single, relatively new members to Peoples Temple. We bonded there, as we worked day and night for a cause we totally believed in.

That was the training ground for us, as we then spread out into other new communes in Redwood Valley. We proved that we could live communally, turn in our income, live very active lives, and stay focused taking on massive amounts of work that needed to be done in the Temple.

Some of the communes had families move in to share housing or had kids move up from other cities to live in the country closer to the Redwood Valley Temple. Some communes were seniors who could combine resources with others so that they had much-improved lifestyles. There was a commune for whatever your desire was, and more and more people saw the benefits of sharing resources.

Most members in the Temple in the early 1970s were conservative, religious folks from Indiana who had moved west, so when we hippie-types hit town and started living successfully in communes, I'm sure they were surprised, and maybe even a bit envious. But Jim Jones was nothing if not a risk-taker. The only exception was in the area of money. He never took any chances there, but rather was extremely tight-fisted with the money. Otherwise, he just pushed by any of the old-timers' reservations and gave us the reins. And we took them and ran with them.

A very surprising part of the communal life in the Temple was that most of us living in the communes were celibate. I'm not sure who was the most surprised – those of us who had been sexually active before joining, or those old-timers who thought of us as "hippies" and didn't know what to make of us. We used our energy for work, for constant work. That and the cold showers were effective in obscuring our sexual drives. Jim preached about taking responsibility and he obviously expected us to act with a conscience. He also introduced us to the concept that our loyalty should be to him, for the cause, and not to a sexual partner. Few of us at the time knew he had different rules for himself.

I lived briefly at East House, the "show commune," across from the Temple building in Redwood Valley. It was given that name because it was the loveliest of the communes with the most manicured lawn, with the nicest furniture, and with what appeared to be sleeping accommodations for six people in the three bedrooms. We put the bedding for the rest of the folks in closets. That was the commune we featured when family members visited, and when out-of-town Peoples Temple members came to look around. My mother came once to visit me when I lived at East House so she saw that commune. After visitors left, and at the end of the long days, we would pull out all the bedding and twelve or fifteen of us would sleep.

Most of us living there were in the "file" group. Besides our full-time jobs and Temple responsibilities like driving buses, doing security shifts around Temple buildings and Jim's house, attending meetings and services Wednesday, Friday, Saturday and Sunday, and counseling Peoples Temple members about family and Peoples Temple issues, managing the files and doing mailings was our area of responsibility. We were held totally responsible for this area. We also had strong mutual respect and love for one another. Of course, we each had our own strengths. Some were peacekeepers, some were organizers, some were endurance role models, some were meticulous workers, and some were "idea" folks. We covered all areas, doing what each of us could do best.

With our chores, we worked diligently to make everything equal. Each person would cook one dinner a week, wash up one night a week, empty trash, clean the bathrooms, vacuum, make lunches, do laundry, or sort laundry, on a regular weekly schedule. I was the popular choice for making the best lunches for us to take to work. My friend Laurie made the best dinners. We worked out the chores efficiently.

Another friend at the house, Andy, had an outside job reading bingo numbers on the six a.m. morning news station. We often made a point of getting up to watch him. One morning, Andy read off bingo numbers and fell asleep, on television, before calling out the next dramatic bingo numbers. We all sat home and laughed hysterically. We considered watching Andy our morning alarm clock. Humor played a big part in our interactions. I firmly believe that people are more humorous than any television show could capture. We laughed a lot, and had very few personality conflicts. We accepted that some very talented people were very peculiar, and worked with that knowledge. There was and is no way to clump our individual personalities into one "type" or one stereotype. There was a lot of banter and a lot of interaction, but mostly about work. We were colleagues working for the same goal. We learned to be hard and careful workers, and to finish our assignments without whining. We weren't freaks; we were just committed members like in any other organization.

My job in the welfare department was tedious at times, but it was satisfying at other times. I worked there before everything was computerized, and we had to write out our narratives about interviews in longhand. Many of my sheets of notes consisted of chicken scratches across the page because I had fallen asleep writing up an interview. My evaluation stated something like, "Good worker but seems to be sleep-deprived." What an understatement!

One evening, I stayed overnight at a care home so that Alice could go to a meeting. When I woke up, I showered and washed my hair and went right to work. It turned out that I had used "relaxer" in my hair, which straightened my already-straight hair. Alice had it for her hair, but I just needed regular shampoo. When I got to work, I had to go into the bathroom, wash my hair with hand soap, dry it with paper towels, hide in the stalls if anyone came in and wait for it to dry. It was an endless process. How did it look? Ridiculous. When I told the story to fellow members, we had a great laugh. There were a lot of laughs because of our ineptitude in being secretive. And we loved a good laugh.

We worked hard, usually 18 hours a day, including our day jobs. All of us, from time to time, would go into the office bathroom to take quick naps in the stalls. Our feet might go to sleep, or we'd have red marks across our foreheads where we'd rested our heads on our arms. We'd have to rub the area or move our tingly feet to get the blood moving again.

Sharon Amos was one of the other Peoples Temple members working at the welfare department. She was a tiny burst of energy, with three children. Her youngest two, Christa and Martin, were beautiful interracial kids. She was one of Jim's personal secretaries and rarely slept. We had an arrangement that during our fifteen-minute breaks, she would go nap in her car. At the correct time, I'd go wake her and take my fifteen-minute nap, and she'd wake me. The absurd thing about that was that we were outside the window of the welfare investigator, who undoubtedly had a big chuckle watching us pretend to be so casual as we went out under his nose to take a nap. He had a great sense of humor and got plenty of laughs from us. My favorite line of his was about my old, beat-up and peeling car. He said that I should take pity on it. If it were a horse, he'd recommend shooting it to put it out of its misery.

Another time, at a welfare staff meeting, the director made some anti-Peoples Temple remark. I walked over to the nearby law office of a Peoples Temple member, and he called the director and got an apology. The director's particular statement had not been true, so we didn't want to let it stand or have more of those kinds of comments made in a public setting without contesting them.

In about 1973, I took over the security at Jim's house. We just had visual surveillance of the area, and we were a bit inept. We didn't carry guns or anything, but we did try to stay awake. His house backed up to railroad tracks and a forested area. The meetinghouse and a few homes of other members were in front of Jim's house, between him and the road. Ukiah and Redwood Valley were both very conservative, mostly white towns. Most of our neighbors were not thrilled and some were dangerously offended. Frankly, though we did have some peculiarities. For instance, Jim had rescued Mr. Muggs, a huge chimpanzee, from a testing lab. His large cage was just behind Jim's house. We built a security tower above Mr. Muggs' cage. Later, we added security to our newly purchased office complex about a mile down the road. I scheduled Temple members to staff both places, with three-hour shifts. I usually took the worst shift – since that way no one whined about having to do a shift. I inevitably stood in the tower, with my eyes open most of the time, from two-five a.m. on Tuesday and Friday mornings. Everyone who was able did security shifts. As I recall, we never had anyone approach Jim's house.

Inside the cabin above Muggs, we had a heater and we could stay inside as long as we could stay awake. Muggs was a fun companion. Once I came and brought my snacks, a banana and an apple. Muggs saw it and made himself look so sad that I gave him the banana. He went into his house and came out with three or four bananas that he had probably conned out of other staffers. He looked like he laughed at me for falling for his scheme. Such a smart guy!

At my commune, when one of my friends was getting out of bed to go to his security post one night, he fell off the top bunk of the three-tiered set of bunk beds. I don't think he was seriously injured, but I know that must have hurt. Our exhaustion took its toll. I remember sleeping so that I stayed a bit cold. That way, it was easier for me to wake up. We slept in sleeping bags on the mattress so that we didn't spend a lot of time on laundry and non-essential household chores. We cleaned up after ourselves because no one got special treatment. No one was more important than anyone else.

As Peoples Temple grew, Jim needed some members to be his hands, eyes, and ears. He set up the Planning Commission in the hierarchy of the Temple.

Laura standing in front of Peoples Temple fleet of greyhound-like buses.

Alice and Ava Ingram

CHAPTER 5
What Were We Planning?

J im had started a leadership sub-group within Peoples Temple in the late 1960s. The Board of Elders included many of the Indiana members and mixed in the newer Mendocino County members. The group was formed to move some of the novice members into more challenging leadership roles and to integrate the newcomers into the Temple's government. Jim didn't always attend himself, but undoubtedly knew everything that was going on in the group. The Board of Elders gradually ceased to function in about 1969.

In the early 1970s, Jim started another internal group called the Planning Commission as a replacement of the Board of Elders. It was eventually known as "PC." In Redwood Valley, PC members were almost exclusively white. However, the group continued to get larger and more integrated over the next few years, and it began to include black and white members from San Francisco and Los Angeles as well. Once the membership was up to sixty or seventy, it was completely integrated. Only Jim's group of personal secretaries remained all white. His ministers and his secretaries for the different Temples in Los Angeles and San Francisco were both black and white.

The Planning Commission included many of the most hard-working members of the Temple, but it was impossible to follow the logic of who was and who wasn't picked to be on the Planning Commission. Many hard workers were NOT on it. The commission was comprised of the old hierarchy, including some of the early Elders, some of the new professionals who had joined, and some of the college students, as well as some of the most committed of the new members in California. It was a status symbol to be on PC, as if you'd been recognized as one of the hardest workers.

I was put on the Planning Commission in late 1972. I had been a self-starter since I walked in the door, and continued to take on more responsibility. My life was very fulfilling to me, and the work with files and with big groups working on deadlines came easy for me. I did my job. Some people were envious about who was put on PC at first, and then saw what rigorous schedules most of us had, and were relieved that they got a pass from that kind of scrutiny. PC usually met at least once a week, for an all-night or late-night session, after the regular meetings. In the early 1970s, we would have a "Family Meeting" for members only on Wednesday nights, and then meetings Saturday night and Sunday morning for everyone. On Sunday night, we'd have a modified "Family Meeting" for those who were regulars. Often after our Wednesday night family meetings, the Planning Commission would re-group at a member's home out in the countryside in Redwood Valley. Redwood Valley was very sparsely populated, and we usually met far off the beaten track so few people would notice the enormous number of cars parked outside a well-lit home, at all hours of the night.

Along with my other responsibilities, I took on a new job in PC, that of "Visitations." Visitations became something all of PC contributed to. During PC meetings, I would pass a list around and people who had some new observations or perspective on what other non-PC members were doing, or hardships they were battling, would jot it down. Later on, I wrote up a report for Jim with all the details about what folks were doing. While I was doing this report, I thought it was understandable that Jim couldn't keep up with all of us, as the Temple membership had exploded. I saw Jim referring to the report during the meetings, from time to time. I didn't think of it as spying at that time. I felt then that Jim was so benevolent, he wouldn't be misusing that information. We would set up counseling sessions, family support, or letter writing campaigns based on Visitations. There were many members helped by others in the Temple who had experience in solving those kinds of problems.

I do have misgivings now, because I have the insight developed over the past thirty years. I think the visitations could have allowed Jim to manipulate some of the members because he had information collected this way. I also remember once during the "healing" ceremony that Jim called a person out but had made a mistake in reading my Visitation report and got the last name wrong. I learned then that not everything was telepathy or clairvoyance, and that he got some help along the way.

I often suspected that his private secretaries did a similar report about those of us on PC and others in the Temple. Since I wasn't in the Temple because of Jim's "gift" I paid no attention to that aspect of his ministry. I was neither threatened nor persuaded by it.

Once in PC, we were told over and over that Jim trusted (and gave positions of prestige) to those who were single – uncoupled. He wanted our undivided attention and adoration. He let us know that if we coupled up, we would be less trustworthy. We all wanted him to have confidence in us, so most people remained celibate. The others were very careful when they went against his admonitions. I didn't know about their activities, but I knew I trusted Jim and did my best. The things going on outside of Peoples Temple didn't tempt me.

Usually in PC, Jim would sit in a comfortable chair and we would surround him in a semi-circle, sitting on the carpet. Sometimes the older members would also sit in chairs off to the side. When I joined, there were about thirty-five members, but the PC increased quickly to over seventy.

The PC meetings included reports on the different areas within Peoples Temple. Jim would ask for an update and the person most on top of a specific area would rise to speak about it. If you were speaking, you would be on the hot seat. If something weren't going well, Jim would let you know. Others with questions would pass them up to Jim, or sometimes ask them. There was a lot of discussion. Problems were solved or identified, and then we'd move on to another topic.

The Planning Commission also served Jim with the opportunity to have a small sampling of feedback on some of his more unorthodox ideas. We were distressed that some of our kids were getting involved in drugs in San Francisco and Los Angeles. We had no way to protect them from the things going on in their communities outside their doors. Since many Temple members and grandparents were raising their grandkids because parents were in jail, absent, or on drugs, we were very concerned. There was a lot of discussion about Guyana in the Planning Commission even before we sent our first group there. The inner cities of the United States were not safe for our children. In his book, *Raven*, Tim Reiterman mentions that Jim visited Guyana in 1962. That was news to me. But Guyana was warm and tropical, was English-speaking, and was racially mixed with black, Indian, Chinese and white. We researched and found that the Guyanese government was anxious to increase the population in the northwest district because of a treaty with Venezuela. We got a lease for land in the middle of the rain forest. Once our first workers were there, we had discussions about Jonestown at every meeting.

Jim also used the PC to talk about revolutionary suicide. Even though he would mention it in the broader services, he talked more frequently and intensely about it in PC. Jim was actually a fountain of ideas. I don't know if he intentionally went off on many tangents or if that was one of his strategies to obscure his main point. I do know that I never felt that revolutionary suicide would be applied to our group. I never had any inkling that he would use those words in November 1978. He was dramatic about so many things that his mentioning it was quickly obscured by his next performance.

During the Planning Commission meetings, Jim truly expected total focus on him. At one gathering, after an exhausting week, and after driving the bus to Los Angeles, I was dozing during our meeting. He was furious. At one point, he took out a small pistol and aimed it at me and told me to wake up. He warned me that if I fell asleep once more, he'd shoot me. I have since talked to others at that same meeting, who had also been nodding off. He had told them the same thing, but I just didn't remember because I was focused on his threat to me, or too tired. In any case, I stayed awake for a few more minutes and then couldn't. He had the bus drivers leave shortly after that. I never thought he would fire the gun, but he did expect total obedience and was furious when anyone did not follow his instruction.

I knew that he was passionate about making the world better, and I knew that it took tremendous dedication and commitment to do it. I just thought his exacting every ounce of my energy was what it would take for us to make our dreams come true. He was a tough taskmaster, like a teacher who pushes you beyond what you thought you could do. He brought out your best. Moderation in commitment was not acceptable. I did not see it as diabolical or dangerous to me, or others, then. He mentioned that Che Guevara didn't slow down, or compromise, that he was 100% revolutionary, 100% of the time. He often mentioned that someone smoking in Che's revolutionary band had brought down Che when the group was hiding out. Someone cost Che his life by doing something so selfish. That was a common theme. How can each help and how can each toe the line of being a revolutionary? Jim would tell us how and when we were not doing our share.

Other times in the Planning Commission, people who had done a job poorly or who had irked Jim in some other way were confronted. I attended PC for about five years, and I recall only twice when someone was actually physically slapped or pushed. But different people were regularly confronted and often humiliated for their behavior. Jim would always set the stage and discuss what action or behavior was intolerable or horrific. By the time the issue was on the floor (in open discussion), we would all be on his side. We weren't physically abused except in those few cases, but Jim was a master of divide-and-conquer tactics. He could whittle down your defenses and peel away your excuses. He would show you and all the others how incompetent you were. Then he'd move on. After dealing seriously with issues, he'd go on to a time of more positive banter. When PC was over, you'd feel like you had a new wind to just do better the next time.

The intensity of the confrontations ebbed and flowed. At times, there was much constructive criticism and many suggestions. There was belittling and humiliation. I never took the brunt of the most devastating, but I saw it too often. We all took our burden of creating a heaven on earth so seriously that we shook off this catharsis and moved forward. I thought that being a revolutionary just had to be hard, and this was hard, so it must be making me a better revolutionary. If I had understood the progression of emotional abuse at that time, I could have been alerted to the effect his strategy was having on us.

Later on, about 1975, the PC meetings became more intense. At one PC meeting, we were on the stage, I recall, in Ben Franklin High School, on Geary near where the SF Temple building was being constructed. Jim gave us some beverage, a first. After we drank it, he said it had been poison because it was time for us to become martyrs in pursuing revolutionary suicide. He had different PC members pretend to fall off chairs to make it look more real. One woman ran out screaming. A few others yelled at Jim. For me, I had always known that Jim was dramatic and that he set a stage for his lessons. I knew or felt I did that it wasn't real, and that he was play-acting. I didn't take it seriously or worry that it might be true. Later, he said that he'd done it to find who was totally committed. I never dreamed we would ever use it.

There were many hoops we were asked to jump through to show our loyalty. Jim tried to prevent future anti-Temple or negative attacks on him from us in PC and in the general congregation, by having us sign blank papers or bogus confessions. I thought I'd always live in the Temple, so I assumed that these were for those who were deceitful, or who would harm Jim and the Temple. As I now write the details from the Temple around 1977, I see so many danger flags. At the time – at all times in the Temple – we were on the move, and we were exhausted. We would never talk to others about our concerns, because our doubts would be brought up publicly. We never actually had pause time to link things to see the whole picture. The good features about life in the Temple were repeated in many settings, and there was a lot of good. But the negative was swept under the rug. Seeing Jim's paranoia and the daily effect it had on us is mind-boggling now.

Jim's management style was complex. In his inner circle, he had a small cadre of white females who assisted him in all of the inner workings, including the obvious and essential things. It turns out that most of them were also his sexual partners. He was the talented, bright, and paranoid leader, and they continued to enable him to take care of business. Even some of these women were trusted more than others, and one of Jim's most masterful efforts was to divide and conquer any peer group. He would create competition for his attention so that no deep alliances were formed within the group. Whatever went on with Jim inside this group was carefully silenced.

Counseling was another job I got when I was put on PC. Counseling in the Temple was helpful to a lot of people. We would have a group of counselors meet with people having any kind of problem, several times a week. The problem could be losing a job, having a sick family member, or being sick yourself, wanting to leave, wanting a divorce, having an affair, having trouble in school, having roommate trouble, or kid or parent troubles. We would talk to all sides and open up communication or take whatever action was necessary. I've come to find out that most churches have some sort of counseling like this. Our counseling wasn't just focused on a religious issue – it could be anything.

From East House, I moved to West House, on West Road in Redwood Valley. About sixteen of us lived there, sleeping in three-tier bunk beds in the bedrooms. I lived there for about two years. It was a big old house on a couple of acres. I loved it there since we had animals and a lot of fun. Many of us worked at the local Welfare Department so we had to be sure that we were careful about what clothes we wore. I couldn't wear a blouse that Laurie or Barbara had worn the day before, or an especially recognizable outfit that would confirm that we were all in Peoples Temple and we all shared our clothing. We did not acknowledge that we were members to anyone on our jobs. However, many people saw us carpool, even when we tried to be secretive and drop folks off or pick them up a few blocks from the office. Our attempt at secrecy was ludicrous but we would never confirm any of the rumors people asked us about.

Secrecy within cults is fairly commonplace. In Peoples Temple, it isolated the membership from others who were not members. Our private lives were never disclosed to the coworkers on our jobs, and we kept relationships on a very superficial level. We never confided anything, from the most obvious to the more private parts, to people outside. Also, we felt more evolved since we working for something heroic, and we were living in humble circumstances. Our time, energy, and money all went to bring about change. We were proud and even judgmental about those who were pursuing possessions and riches. We isolated ourselves by feeling superior, and different than those in the world around us.

Another of my jobs in the Temple was as a "Greeter." Before each service, a number of us, some PC, some not, would wait out in front of the Temples, or whatever building we were using for our service that day, and interview new attendees. We would get names and addresses. If they had never attended, we would draw them aside and a few of us would "tell them about the service" and find out how they got there, and what they were expecting. We were looking to get a general feeling from them if they were friend or foe. If they were white or rich looking, we would be more careful about sizing them up. If they seemed antagonistic or hostile, we would pass a note back to Jim and he would let us know when to send them away, explaining that we'd invite them back another day. If they seemed genuinely harmonious, curious, open, politically motivated, or liberal, we would note that and send it back to Jim. We got to be expert at the process after several times a week for several years. We sort of gravitated towards those who stood out, and did our own profiling. Some days, Jim would want only returning members and family. Some days, he took everyone and his sermon would cover the whole gamut of his theology. Our job was to keep out hostile folks. There were about twenty of us, at least, who would serve as greeters. I liked it because I met some great people that way. I also liked the challenge of interviewing people to find their real motivation in coming. It also kept me in touch with many in the Peoples Temple family who lived in the different cities.

One of the reasons I was happy in the Temple was because of the variety of jobs I could do. My life rushed by and I had a ball. I was happy, invigorated and challenged. It was never dull, and each day brought new unexpected experiences.

At this same time, some were hoarding money so that they could leave the Temple with some resources. Some were having sexual liaisons. Some were going out to movies and restaurants. The zealots (me and many others) thought movies or paying to go out to dinner was frivolous. Many of us would get our meager allowance and donate it back to the Temple, or buy the delicious homemade food sold after services on Sundays. We were purists and intolerant of those less committed. Those who did go out never talked about it. I've heard that sometimes people would go out and see other members at the restaurants or at the movies. I had no clue that they were doing these things. I never made those choices for several reasons. I didn't want to spend the money, I didn't have the time, my other work would not get done, and I might get caught. For the most part, I hung out with the straight-and-narrow group of people who were energetically doing their jobs. I don't know what would have happened if I had decided to do otherwise. I think I would have just left the Temple. I wasn't interested then, and am not interested now, in subterfuge. That may be because my life was so wasted just before I joined and I was ready for something more meaningful. Whatever my reasons were, I am still surprised when I speak with other survivors who strayed in this way.

One of the most fulfilling tasks that Jim took on was our care for the elderly, primarily in San Francisco. The Temple provided meals during the week for seniors. In addition to that, after services on most weekends, the lawyers, nurses, accountants, and social workers would meet with people to help fill out forms, give advice, share information, and write appeal letters. It was extremely helpful to people on welfare who were required to fill out complex forms for minimal support. If the forms were done incorrectly, the people would be punished with long delays. We helped people with disability insurance forms, and social security forms, and we also collected information about relatives in jail or relatives facing charges. We would then circulate the information and write multitudes of letters to judges, or to other officials, to get charges lessened or dropped.

We had a telephone tree so that one person would call five and those five would each call their five, and so on, to get a message around. That functioned to alert people to send letters to people who were sick or in dire straights, to gather helpers for someone, or to rally members to show up at a demonstration or public relations event. We had a very efficient communication system. That was used a lot when Jim wanted us to demonstrate somewhere or if a political candidate was to be wooed. A quick call around San Francisco could bring hundreds in a very short time. People would come on our buses or come by local transportation.

Our membership had blossomed and we had nearly a thousand dedicated members in San Francisco and nearly the same in Los Angeles. New people continued to come, primarily hoping for a healing. But there was a solid core group in each city that did an enormous amount of work in taking care of the other members and of us when we drove in on the buses each week or two.

Finally, in late 1975 or so, I moved into my own office on the ground floor of the business property that we purchased on East Road. I slept on an old door with a sleeping bag on top. I still worked on my day job, but while there, I worked with the tapes of Jim's weekly radio broadcasts. The tapes would be made of each of his radio sermons and

I would index and store them. I also spent time with staff opening and responding to prayer requests and letters to Jim. People sent donations and ordered Jim's prayer cloths. I still ran security at both Jim's house and at that office location. By that time, the business property housed our "letters" office, the print shop, the storage room for all the tapes I was organizing, three small bedrooms off of one office, a large supply building in the back, a laundromat we managed, and three apartments upstairs for Temple members.

The whole time I was in Peoples Temple, I turned in my paycheck and got an allowance. If I needed basic things, I could get them at our Temple store for free, things like soap, shampoo, underwear, socks, or deodorant. If I needed to buy something like shoes, I'd turn in the receipt and get reimbursed. We recycled everything. If any clothes were too big or small, I would return them to the Temple store that Helen Swinney managed, and take what I needed from someone else's recycled goods. It worked fine. We often cited parts of the Bible when we were out in the community. One of our favorites was in Matthew 25. The Lord was asked when was he seen hungry or thirsty, and he replied that whatever was done for the least of his brothers was done for him. We preached about it and did it. We knew that caring for poor people was an important part of our lives. We were not wasteful of our resources, and we had rich, fulfilling lives. The number or quality of possessions is not what determines that richness of purpose.

These little vignettes show what we were about. We were not interested in acquiring wealth, in being popular, or in fitting in. We were "in this world but not of it." We loved that we were working for a better world, working our butts off, and that every moment moved us along that path. These were exhilarating days. We had fun while we were working so hard. We felt like we were working for a just cause, and there was never a dull moment.

During this time, while those of us in Redwood Valley worked hard, and focused our attention on the "heaven on earth" we hoped for, Jim expanded his empire into San Francisco and Los Angeles. Poor people flocked to the Temple for the services we offered and we continued providing free meals, free legal advice, free social worker advice, counseling for kids and grandkids in the home, and letters to be written to judges where loved ones were in trouble with the law.

Politicians came because throngs of people were there. The word got around about Jim and Peoples Temple. Jim could pull off a big political meeting in no time, and fill the seats, or leaflet, or demonstrate. He had many resources at his disposal. Politicians loved him. Soon after being elected, Mayor George Moscone appointed Jim as head of the San Francisco Housing Authority.

When we went to San Francisco and Los Angeles, many of us would go out and panhandle, to "Feed the World's Children" – as we told contributors—adding money to the Peoples Temple coffers. Buses would take us and pick us up. We'd go whenever there was time before or after meetings or other events. We always had a competition to see who could collect the most. I fully believed that the money was going to feed the world's hungry children. The pictures that we had taped around our cans were of starving kids in Africa, but I knew for sure that we were feeding hungry of all ages, in cities of America. I didn't know exactly if Jim was sending money elsewhere, but I saw that he was definitely feeding the hungry.

Beginning with trips in July and December of 1971, Jim took national bus trips to the East Coast and Indiana. He would load up the buses, at least six or seven, for these trips. We were efficient travelers. There was a nurse on each bus along with all the food supplies and other necessary equipment. Everyone was invited to go, and no matter how young or old, everyone was accommodated. Many retired seniors in their eighties would go for the ride. We traveled all around the country from Texas, to Louisiana, to Florida, and then through Memphis, and Atlanta to Washington, D.C., Baltimore, Philadelphia, Chicago, Indiana and back to California.

We traveled from city to city and meeting location to the next meeting location without sightseeing, except for one trip through Washington, D.C., when we stopped at some of the monuments. Our housing was arranged and many stayed in local churches, or in relatives' homes, sleeping in sleeping bags on the floor. For me, it was pure delight. I met people from every city and shared food and space with them. I felt included and delighted to be able to meet these thoughtful people.

We drivers would have a bus assigned and then bring our sleeping bags. We'd take a driving shift and then take a shift sleeping in the luggage compartments under the bus. If it was hot out, we could leave the luggage door latched but open, to get some air. If it were cold, we'd bring extra blankets. If we needed to use the bathroom, we'd knock on the ceiling and people on the bus would tell the driver, and the caravan would pull into the next rest stop. We tried to plan ahead so that we didn't have to count on that for pit stops. There were too many "ifs." If the bus was quiet enough for people to hear you knock, if the people on the bus weren't asleep, if the driver wasn't talking to the other drivers on the radio, if there was a restroom close by where 250-300 people could use facilities, so we tried to plan ahead. Some ingenious drivers created their own suites under the bus and put their own real mattress, music, and speakers. When I finally got under the bus, all I wanted was sleep so that is what I did.

Riding in those compartments was undoubtedly illegal and/or unhealthy. It was one of the many experiences I had in the Temple that could never happen elsewhere. There was always something unexpected coming around the corner. It was never, never dull. On top of the bus, seniors had seats, kids were in the luggage racks, others were in the hallways – the buses were always packed. They could be silent, with people sleeping, or loud, right after a vibrant meeting. But since drivers had to get sleep to be safe on the next leg of the trip, we got these special accommodations.

Sometimes, I would leave the Temple cross-country caravan and take a Greyhound back home. Once, I took the Greyhound across country to see my mom in Washington, D.C. I went as a surprise and I can remember now washing my hair in the Washington, D.C. Greyhound bus terminal bathroom so that I didn't smell like the bus. On one such trip going back to California from the east, I was traveling with my friend, Bobby Stroud. We pretended that we were a stranded brother and sister. When we got to Las Vegas, we were able to get a sandwich. We thought the people there were generally more generous that those in the Midwest, where no one would even think of helping out.

When I wasn't driving a bus on these trips, I would often go on the "Advance Crew." A group of six or eight of us would head out in a van filled with tens of thousands of flyers. We would have housing with a family member of someone in the Temple, or sometimes, we'd stay in churches that Jim had connected with. We'd get to the cities where Jim was going to have services, and we'd pass out thousands of leaflets printed by our print shop. We'd go only to black communities. It was very hard work. Generally, we'd drive non-stop, with each person taking a three-hour shift driving. Then we'd hand out all the flyers and move on to the next city and do the same thing. The Advance Crew was also fun. We had hours to talk and laugh and just travel along. We met wonderful people who housed us along the way. Sharing homes with people, either on long bus trips, or in San Francisco, Los Angeles, Seattle, or elsewhere, was a highlight for me. As a single white woman, there would have been very few ways for me to have that rich and lovely experience. The Temple opened doors for us with all colors mixing with all colors. I miss that sharing and inclusion very much.

One summer, we were in Chicago, in a high-rise housing project. The elevator wasn't working and it was very hot. Chicago was always either freezing or steaming. I always hated going there to hand out pamphlets. In the housing projects, we would each take a floor to pass out flyers and then race each other to the opposite stairs. Looking back, I see that that was a bit risky, but at the time, it was expedient. After we came down from one particular project, we packed up and went home. That night, the news showed that a woman was thrown off the top floor of the same project and landed near to where we had parked. We were very stunned after that. We had literally just left that project, but we felt immune to that kind of violence and danger because of our mission there.

Jim always had his services in very poor parts of major cities. Our job was to leaflet those same areas. We never had any incident, but our (always) interracial group stood out in many of the areas we worked in. I don't know if an all-white neighborhood would have been as kind in all parts of the country. In Texas, we integrated the front seat of the cars we drove in and we had some close calls because we rode like this. I remember feeling myself to be in danger several times in Texas and I was always glad to leave and travel north. When I was in Texas, I never entertained the idea of visiting my father. There was no way he would have ever understood what I was doing or why I was traveling in Texas in an integrated group, acting like sisters and brothers. No explanation would have made him see it my way. Besides that, our time wasn't our own. We were there for a purpose and that took all of our energy and time to finish and move on.

In letters to Jim, people told him of healings that they had received after meetings, or when they had asked him for a blessing, or had bought some of his religious photos or prayer cloths. There was a Letters office where all of these letters were received and answered. Part of the ongoing responsibility of the files and printing crews was to send out mailings offering items that could be used as "blessings." The print shop would send out little red square prayer cloths, pictures of Jim with the children or healing someone. There were all sorts of advertising items from pens to photos. People could buy them and then make contributions to the ministry. These donations made up a huge part of the budget. The Mertle family was the most instrumental in getting this advertising department off the ground. Their ideas were amazingly creative. After the Mertle family left Peoples Temple, they went on to form "Concerned Relatives," a group of disenchanted former members and relatives of current Peoples Temple members.

In the mid-1970s, our band director and music creator arranged for us to make a record. For four or five weeks, up to thirty of us would go to a recording studio and record some of our music. We had a great time spending relaxing time together while we waited all over the building. We had to be available so that any moment when the soloists weren't being recorded, we could go up and do the group numbers. The record came out well, and the process was exciting. The album was called <u>He's Able</u> and some of our best singers were recorded. I wish we had professionally taped more of our music!

In late 1974, I had another "first" in Peoples Temple.

CHAPTER 6
My First Trip to Paradise-1974

I learned a lot about building a community in the rain forest. After you find the perfect location, you draw up your plans. When the first members of Peoples Temple went to Guyana to look at the land, the government instructed us to build in the northwest region. This was a disputed border area between Guyana and Venezuela. Guyana had ten years to develop the region and significantly increase the population. Otherwise, Venezuela would have some rights to that region. The area picked for Jonestown was thick rain forest with many crisscrossing footpaths, which the Amerindians used to move about. There were thick forests, which could be cut and prepared for crops, and windrows (deep crevices or ravines in the earth) filled with some rocks and roots, where the water would run off.

In December 1973, a small group traveled to Guyana to find a home for us. In February 1974, Peoples Temple and the government of Guyana co-signed a lease for land in the northwest district.

Once we had selected the area, we moved ahead with help from local experts and workers, and the Guyanese government. Meeting the challenge of making the rain forest into a home is hard work. First you have to cut down the huge trees. After that, you have to use a backhoe and remove all the deep roots and trunks. Then you have to burn everything. Once everything is burned and ashy, you have to plow the field and mix the rich topsoil and the ashes. Since it rains on a nearly daily basis, all of this takes a long time.

A small group of very hard-workers took on that task. Joyce and Charlie Touchette were there with their sons, as well as some other "experts" who had come from the ranks of Peoples Temple. The community was tiny, but the work was getting done. More workers arrived in June 1974. It was extremely tedious, and sometimes boring, work. Several large fields had been prepared for crops, and other areas were clear at the center of the property.

Two of the early settlers left Jonestown and Peoples Temple around that time. They were too isolated in the interior of Guyana, since it was twenty-four hours by boat from Georgetown. It would have been difficult for many people. Also, the Touchette clan was fairly dominant and very skilled at using all of the equipment, so as a group, they directed the project and organized the work. The Touchette family was close-knit and powerful. Those outside of the family could have felt very isolated in the small community of Jonestown. These committed people moved to the middle of the rain forest and worked tirelessly getting the community ready for the influx.

In 1974, at Christmastime, I had my first trip to Guyana. Jim took PC and some others to take a look at the location of our "Promised Land." The church paid for everything. We rented a private plane, and Norman Ijames, the pilot son of AJ, flew us to Guyana. We flew into Georgetown and then took an interior flight to Matthew's Ridge. Then we took trucks and land rovers into the Peoples Temple Agricultural Project. When we arrived at the front gate, there was a deeply rutted dirt road for several miles into the area where we had started our community. We passed what would develop into our piggery on the right-hand side, about a mile from the front gate. We kept going into the area that had been carved out of the rain forest. There were several solid wood buildings, and many acres of leveled ground. They were at different stages of the process to make them ready to plant.

Jim and the rest of us stayed for several days, slept out in the rain forest, saw the progress, and heard the glowing reports. I loved the country, the people I'd met, and the excitement of seeing the project. I don't remember having any doubts that I'd find a place for myself there. Even though it was a world away from any of the experiences I'd had in my first thirty years, I felt hugged by the rain forest, and by the tropics.

While there, we took turns doing security around the equipment and the piggery. We had no guns so we just stayed awake all night, talking to friends, so that no one would come up and take our things. I delighted in sitting up at night, in the tropics, listening to the forest. I can remember seeing a wild cat sitting up on the seat of one of our heavy equipment tractors watching us. I guess he thought he was scheduled for security too. One night, while walking to the piggery to do security, we picked lemon grass and made lemon grass tea as we sat around in the piggery. Two people would always do security together. We just stayed on site, but still slept there. The assumption was that we'd wake up if someone or some animal came around.

When we finally had to leave, we took the Cudjoe (our larger boat) into Georgetown. I was enchanted by the twelve hours in inland waterways, heading to the ocean. We would wave at the Amerindians as we floated by, just appreciating the loveliness of nature and the tropics. Birds would be flying in front of us, we'd pass canoes, and animals, and just everything about it was lovely. The boat spent the last 12 hours on the ocean, docking in Georgetown. It was a bit rough. Some on the boat got seasick and as a result, their memories are much more negative than mine.

I loved Georgetown also. To me, it had such a rich and vital air about it. All races moved together. The nation had rebuffed the British rule, and had become independent in the 1950s. The leadership was black, East Indian and Chinese. There was a sprinkling of other races – but the whole culture seemed so rich and inclusive, and so interesting to experience. I hadn't found anything about Guyana not to like.

We came home and went back to our jobs. In the Temple, we kept our news and our activities to ourselves. Some of the non-Temple neighbors in Ukiah and Redwood Valley had some clues about us, but only about the most superficial parts of our lives. Most of our co-workers never knew we had gone to Guyana. I had gotten a smallpox vaccination before going, and remember I had to come up with some excuse about why I had the scar on my arm when I returned. We settled back in at home, but our hearts and minds had already moved to Guyana.

Laura and Terri Carter Jones in front of the plane on the 1974 trip to Jonestown.

CHAPTER 7
A Tropical Destination

The Peoples Temple Agricultural Project was steadily growing. Jim had frequent collections in all the stateside services and had hundreds of members living communally and turning in their paychecks. That number was growing steadily. Many of the people who had just been getting by on Social Security or disability checks had a much richer lifestyle than before by sharing resources, by getting the free meals, and by availing themselves of the free legal and medical consultation offered by the Temple. Other members donated homes and valuables. Jim was a master at taking offerings. All of the development in Jonestown, expenses in and around the Temple buildings in Redwood Valley, San Francisco, and Los Angeles, and expenses of traveling and maintaining an active, exploding church were covered by these donations. Still, more people sent in donations to get Jim's blessing for themselves or their loved ones. Jim was a hands-on manager and was very sparing with spending any money on non-essentials.

A Peoples Temple friend was scheduled to go to Guyana but she had just left the welfare department and was working in San Francisco, in a somewhat prestigious job. Jim realized she couldn't leave and called me in to see him. He told me I was leaving for Guyana in five days. My life was more wonderful than my wildest dream – for all the opportunity in the Temple. I still saw racism, bullying, and horrific crimes against humanity going on all around me in the world. But I wasn't going to just sit and watch it. I was able to leave it behind. Those were my thoughts.

Twelve of us drove from California to Florida, and then we flew into Guyana. The members who were immigrating staggered the trips so that no one would take note of so many people fleeing to Guyana. We left from many different airports around the country. Most of the folks who came with me traveled immediately out to Jonestown on the Cudjoe, our boat. I stayed in Georgetown for the first few months.

After the mosquitoes of Georgetown had taken all they wanted of my blood, I wasn't much bothered by them. At the beginning, I was all blotchy with mosquito bites. I was glad they moved on to the next victim relatively soon after I got there. I never had a problem with them in Jonestown, but in Georgetown, they worked as a team and covered any exposed part. Since it was warm, there were many exposed parts of all of us.

I grew up in Washington, D.C., where we had snow days each year. I hate to be cold. When I got to Guyana, I thought I had gone to heaven. (And I don't even believe in heaven.) The tropics have rich smells, colors, sounds, and culture, in truth, such a great diversity of experiences. I immediately fell in love with the country and the people.

In Georgetown, I was a "procurer." My job included buying all mechanical parts needed for Jonestown equipment, acquiring all food for the Jonestown (and Georgetown) Peoples Temple residents, and buying all supplies – shoes, glasses, clothing, and soaps, just everything. I also went door-to-door, getting donations. If someone had a special request-for example once Jim needed a magnifying glass-I would try to get it donated.

Another job I had was to purchase hundreds, even thousands, of shoes from the manager of the Bata Shoe Store. I procured fish from the main fishery in Georgetown. The owner allowed us to go on his commercial fishing vessel after he off-loaded most of his catch. We would come on board at night, work all night cleaning the remaining fish, and then store them in his freezer until the Cudjoe came back to town and could take them into Jonestown.

I also traveled all over the coastal parts of Guyana. I traveled to the areas of Berbice, where they grew the most beautiful and sweet pineapples, and into the canals where there were huge, high coconut palms. I bought fruits and vegetables at the farmer's markets and from vendors. I frequently went to the abattoir and purchased sides of beef and pork to ship to Jonestown. I bought rice and ramen-like noodles, eggs, coffee, fruit, flour, tea, plants, and food I had never heard of.

My life in Georgetown also included picking people up at the airport, taking people to medical appointments, getting everyone residency status (forms and interviews) before they went out to Jonestown, writing thank-you notes for donations, and monitoring some radio coverage in the Georgetown house that required taking notes of ham radio handles so that we could send them the Jonestown and Georgetown ham radio post cards. I had the additional jobs of maintaining some medical records, picking up and dropping off packages at the government offices, visiting with dignitaries (usually with a group), traveling in search of bulk food, loading the Cudjoe, participating in public relations with other Georgetown residents, doing chores around the house and office, and picking up mail deliveries. It was hard, even grueling, most of the time. We operated on a shoestring budget, and never made purchases without Jim's explicit approval.

I worked in these areas from March 1977 until about March 1978. I would take occasional trips into Jonestown, and then come back to Georgetown. I remember my friend, Paula Adams, describing the trip on the Cudjoe as "awesome." That was before the word was so over-used. We felt like we shared such rich lives, living in that paradise.

My best Guyanese friends in Georgetown were people I met during this time. I corresponded with several of them after I returned to the United States. I got scrap metal donated from an extremely kind, generous man who owned Gooding's Metal Works. He befriended those of us working in Georgetown, and later even briefly housed one of the other survivors until she could fly back to the United States.

The Guyanese were extremely generous. They would serve us tea with condensed milk, or juice made with tropical fermented star fruit and cane sugar, and they'd be gracious hosts whenever we had time to pause in our hectic days. They'd invite us for dinner and embrace us. Sometimes, we'd have curry, which I developed an addiction for. We would have chicken in their special recipe of "chicken in the blanket," which was chicken wrapped in their delicious bread called "roti." I never threw away a cup of coffee. If I poured it in the morning, I would drink it whenever I got home. It was just too delicious.

Georgetown was a poor city, but there were many rich people there, too. It had a relatively simple life. I remember often thinking about the incongruity of me driving (haphazardly and quickly) through town in the Peoples Temple van, while horse-drawn wagons took up much of the road. Although there were cars, most people rode the twenty-five-cent taxis. You'd hop into a cab, already crowded with five or more others and, for twenty-five cents, you'd get dropped off at the corner near your destination. The most vicious crime there was the "choke-and-rob." Someone might come up behind you, put you in a chokehold, and take your wallet. In the end we brought the worst crime to that lovely country, so much worse than any of their choke-and-rob criminals.

One of the loveliest pictures I have in my mind is that of the school children flooding out of school on their way home. They looked like flower blossoms cascading down the street in lovely bright colors, with all different skin tones. They were all talking, laughing, and frolicking. It was an exceedingly touching sight. I was in love with Guyana and the Guyanese people, in addition to being in Peoples Temple and loving what I was doing there.

By the summer of 1977, more and more Peoples Temple members began immigrating to Guyana. The airport was over an hour from the house, and almost all the flights came in late at night. We just had one van. I picked up people at the airport, walked them through customs, and took them into Georgetown, to our house at Lamaha Gardens. I often had to make two or three trips to get everyone there. Each group also brought many heavy duffle bags filled with Jonestown necessities. The van was always packed. The influx of new people brought a lot more work to everyone. Jonestown wasn't yet self-sufficient, and I had to buy more food, and more supplies, along with doing a lot to process the newcomers.

In early 1978, as I was going around "procuring," I met up with a pharmacist in Georgetown. We struck up a friendship. He said that he could gather a few other friends and they could all go out to pick up a new, huge batch of Temple members flying in from California. So, we did it. It was great. One caravan picked up everyone and everything. I was delighted.

One evening after that, the pharmacist and I went out. I don't remember how I excused myself from the house, but I did. We had sex. When I got back to the house, I was confronted and admitted it.

I never did have a poker face, and I hadn't prepared myself to lie about it. I guess I was just as surprised as anyone else. I had been celibate for six years, working my tail off for the cause I loved. There had been a lot of things I hadn't had time for, including sleep, sex, daydreaming, plotting, and whining, just a lot of things. I was rather astonished by the turn of events.

As a result of my infraction of the rules, I got immediately relocated to Jonestown. As soon as I got to Jonestown, I was called up front at a public meeting. Jim told me he was disappointed in me, and said, "I should have slept with you myself." I do remember cringing at that thought. A couple of people slapped me, and I was put on the PSC, the Public Services Crew. Marthea Hicks was the supervisor at the time. She was a tough taskmaster. On the crew, we ran from place to place, did everything in a group, worked longer hours than the rest of the residents and had no free time. The crew was filled with people who had broken some rule or other. Our sentences were determined by the gravity of our crime. After a couple of weeks, Marthea moved on, and I became the supervisor, which was the way things went on the PSC. After a bit, someone else took that job, and I became a crew leader over a group that picked greens out of the windrow, planted and maintained crops, picked vegetables, and dug up starches for the kitchen workers to prepare for our communal meals. We were feeding nearly a thousand people, three meals a day.

One thing that always got our attention would be when we were working in the fields and one of us would feel one single drop of water. We'd call out to each other and run as fast as our legs would carry us to a storage shed or any other cover. If we had more than one hundred yards to go, we might not make it before the monsoonal rains swept through. It was a race for us. Even if we got wet, the sun that followed the rain would dry us off, but it was harder getting our socks and the insides of our shoes dry. In the tropics, athlete's foot and fungus were always a problem. We would love the sprint and the short respite and, we'd talk and laugh for the duration. It was a time of great camaraderie.

Guyana has huge bumblebees. They were so big they defied gravity. We called them B-22s. Sometimes they would fly into us because it seemed that they did not have the ability to change directions easily. That would entertain us also. We learned to not be afraid of the snakes in the tropics. Someone with experience told us that if snakes hear you coming and have a chance to get away, they would slide away. They only strike when they are surprised. We were always noisy, especially after that, so no one was ever bitten by a snake in Jonestown.

Our daily schedule on the crew was to wake up, and have breakfast in the dining area. My crew and I would then gather big burlap bags and quickly go out and collect ten or twelve full bags of greens or some other vegetable. After that, we'd set the bags on our heads and carry them all back to the kitchen where the seniors would clean and prepare them for lunch or dinner. We'd scoop up our sack lunches and head back out to dig cassava, eddoes, sweet potatoes, or some other starch to be used for dinner. Once our meals were covered, we would get into planting or maintaining other crops. We might plant sweet potatoes, or we might weed some plants we had planted earlier in the year. We also might make soap, cut brush, or carry water out to new seedlings. In the late afternoon, we would head back in. Often we'd eat and then go shower. I can remember trying to save myself a trip by putting my shampoo in my hair back at my cottage so that I would shower and keep on going over to the pavilion. There were always events in the evenings.

Jim spoke over the speaker for several hours every day. He would also play the international news broadcasts. He wanted to be kept informed and so did we. Jonestown was very remote, and we all felt we wanted more connection with what was going on far away. He frequently spoke about taking the entire group to the Soviet Union. He told us that no one from the United States would bother us there. We had a plan to take a friendship tour to the Soviet Union and present a Talent Show. From early in his ministry Jim insisted that every group doing anything or going anywhere should be integrated. I was in the singing group, but he had Shirley Smith try to help me sing "with rhythm." She was only partially successful. But we certainly had a lot of challenging practice time while she gave it her best shot. It was wonderful to be singing such heart-felt and often original songs. We had extremely talented musicians and singers in the Temple and their creative sides blossomed in Jonestown.

When I finished practice, I'd teach Spanish to the kids, or discuss politics with groups of adults, or I'd type some projects for Dick Tropp, who had gathered residents' resumes to be submitted to the Soviet embassy. A group of us generally stayed up, had a midnight snack of thick soup or something, and then worked a bit more. Then we'd go to bed. I did that for eight months.

During our meetings in the Pavilion, one of the fascinating things Jim set up was breast exams. There were many more women than men in Jonestown. Every six months or so, our nurses and doctors would set up tables at the back of the Pavilion. All the women in Jonestown would go back and just cycle through. The whole process was very matter-of-fact and quick. There was no issue of modesty or shyness. It was a routine that we appreciated and understood, because our health was important. The doctors and nurses would do the breast exams. If there were any concerns about a lump, the doctor would come over and make some decision. We had the well-stocked medical unit in Jonestown, but we often sent people to Georgetown or even into Caracas, Venezuela, for more complicated medical treatment.

The Amerindians of the Northwest District used our hospital all the time. They would come in for pre-natal tests and everything else. Once, a poisonous snake bit a young Amerindian boy. His parents brought him to us, but we couldn't give him the care he'd need for some reason. Either it was too late, or other drugs were needed. In any case, arrangements were made for a plane to come from Georgetown that very night to pick him up. We drove all of our vehicles to the Kaituma airstrip and parked them all around the airstrip with the headlights on, to provide enough light for the plane to land and then take off. So many of the inventions and the responses to our needs in Jonestown were ingenious!

One of my favorite inventions was that our bakers had rigged up an oven that would bake bread on one side and dry our laundry on the other. None of our energy was to be wasted.

Another unique creation was the bathrooms. They were modified outhouses, that is, boards over a hole dug deep in the ground underneath, but with accommodations for six or eight people at a time and no stalls. I remember some of my best conversations were there and I suppose it was because that was one place where you could actually sit still. From time to time, as necessary, those communal outhouses would be relocated and the original hole covered over. We used charcoal and ashes to keep the smell down. We used the ashes from the areas we cleared and burned for that and to make soap, which we then sold and also used ourselves.

Another innovation was our underground refrigeration unit. We had generators to actually keep it even cooler, but there in the tropics, we had dug a very deep cavern, deep enough for our trucks to get in and out. It kept our food from spoiling. We had to keep an enormous amount of food on hand. Jonestown was still several years away from being self-sufficient and producing enough food even at the end. We also experimented with making our own feed for the pigs in the piggery, planting hill rice as grown in parts of China, and irrigating land if we had just planted an area and no rain had come for a substantial period of time. Members became innovative because ordering things and waiting to receive them was time-consuming and expensive. It reminded me of the reputation of the Cubans. They are the best at repairs and finding alternative solutions to car problems because the U.S. blockade has made many automotive parts inaccessible. There was no choice but to improvise. So we did.

The housing in Jonestown was based on health and age. The older members or those with health problems that kept them from walking some distance lived in the center, near all the facilities. Those of us who were younger and healthier lived out in the cottages. The housing for the seniors was in several big dorms with bunk beds. Many people strung up sheets to have a little more privacy. There were at least sixty people in each dorm. A few seniors had such severe health issues that they had their own cottages. Pop and Mom Jackson lived in one. Pop was one of the oldest and feistiest residents. He took great pride in the garden around his cottage, and still studied about hill rice, peanuts, and other ideas to expand the crops grown in Jonestown. The seniors moved around some as they were in tight quarters and personality conflicts arose in the dorms.

I lived out in the far cottages. We continued to build cottages and were up to fifty-three by November 1978. I lived in Cottage 48 and shared one side of the loft with Phyllis Chaikin. On the other side were Chris Rozynko and Shirley Hicks. Sometimes I thought we had brought California earthquakes with us to Guyana. Downstairs, there were four sets of bunk beds. I was only ever in my cottage to sleep, but I do remember waking to the sight of the sun rising over the eastern vista of the rain forest. It was as lovely a sight as I have ever seen. I loved the expressiveness of the sky in Guyana. If a storm were coming, the sky would yell at you to take cover. If the sun was about drying things up, you could almost see it smile.

Often when I walked toward the pavilion, I would pass Bea Orsot and Tom Grubbs' cottage, and their dog Trixie would come out and greet me. Trixie was one of the few personal animals in Jonestown. We did have others, though. Besides big old Mr. Muggs, we had a sloth – a slow-moving, confused animal—and Jake, our anteater. Some of the kids would take Jake on walks to huge anthills where he could eat 10,000 ants in one scoop of his long tongue. We also had lovely toucan, a few pet scorpions, and another monkey or two.

For us, things were about to change. I couldn't have anticipated the difference a few weeks would make.

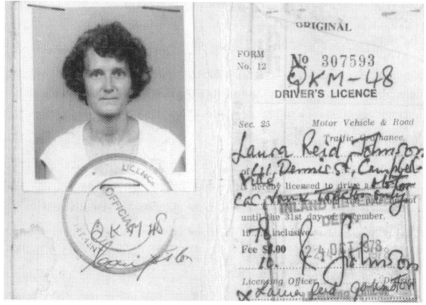

Laura's Guyanese Drivers; License

CHAPTER 8
Georgetown and Survival

One evening in October 1978, in Jonestown, Jim called me in to meet with him. He told me that some of the folks working in Georgetown needed a break and wanted to come into Jonestown for some time off. He asked if I could I keep my act together, and return to Georgetown. I said yes. He told me he was sending me in for the next two-to-three weeks, and then I'd come back. I said fine. Since arriving in Guyana in March 1977, I had been delighted by everything I'd seen. In Georgetown, I had enjoyed my time working there and socializing with friends I met along the way. I was awfully pleased with the prospects of returning to the capital city and some of my old responsibilities. In Jonestown, we had hard work and camaraderie with our Temple family. In Georgetown, we had hard work and new experiences because we were living in a different country and different culture. Both locations were fulfilling for me.

That same night after leaving Jim, I remember going to the community store, and seeing Alice Ingram. She had been one of my best friends in Redwood Valley and continued to be one of my dearest friends in Jonestown. I remember that evening's conversation with Alice very well. We talked about my going back to Georgetown. She shared my happiness that I was sort of "forgiven" and was able to move back and forth to Georgetown as the job dictated. She got me all set up with city clothes and things I'd need. I always felt that Alice was like my sister. She didn't put up with nonsense. She was direct and strong. She laughed a lot, and was fairly quiet. But she had a look that would kill you. There was no way to misinterpret her "look." She had been my friend since I had first hooked up with Chris Lewis, and she had always been my ally. She seemed to be at peace, well placed in the store where she could monitor supplies and make sure people were taken care of. She was an exceptionally hard worker, and once her mind was set, there was no wiggle room!

I packed up my sparse belongings, and left for Georgetown the next day or so. I picked up my life there just where I had left off and never did meet up with the pharmacist again. I was in Georgetown from late October through and beyond November 18.

Those of us living in Guyana outside of Jim's inner circle were mostly oblivious to the shifting winds of opinions about Peoples Temple outside of Guyana. In California, newspapers were beginning to break through the protective wall that surrounded the Temple. Relatives became alarmed that their family members picked up all their belongings and left the country. Concerned Relatives began speaking with the media and with elected officials about claims of abuse and brainwashing. Some families in the midst of custody battles saw the kids in question relocating to Guyana. Tim and Grace Stoen were contesting custody of their son, John, who was living in Jonestown. They had both left Peoples Temple, but Jim was not allowing John Stoen to return to them. Jim contended that he was actually John's father and maintained that he had parental rights. Grace had spoken to government officials, as had another Temple member who had fled from Jonestown. The custody hearing in Guyana was in the process of addressing John's custody.

California Congressman Leo Ryan was beginning to hear about these charges. Then, Congressman Ryan's friend and constituent, Sam Houston, spoke to him about his own son and his involvement with Peoples Temple. Bob Houston, his wife Phyllis, and their two children Patty and Judy, were Peoples Temple members. Bob left the Temple but he wanted continued contact with his daughters. He was working in some capacity on the train, in the Bay Area. Soon after he left the Temple, he was killed in an accident on his job. It appeared that he fell asleep while working and was killed in a fall. While in Peoples Temple, Bob had suffered from narcolepsy, and I had seen him frequently fall asleep in the most peculiar locations and positions. To this day, I don't believe that anyone in Peoples Temple had anything to do with this death, although others disagree with me. There were many who presented a major threat to Peoples Temple's independence and relocation, yet there were no other deaths. However, Bob's children and his ex-wife had moved immediately to Guyana. There was definitely a custody fight brewing and Bob's father asked Congressman Ryan to help protect his grandchildren.

At Jim's instruction, some people who had left the Temple were threatened and intimidated against going public about any concerns. I have never heard of anyone touched, much less killed. I only learned about the threats from some fellow survivors and from some who were threatened. But, I knew nothing about it then, and couldn't have imagined it.

After research and interviews with Concerned Relatives, ex-members, and other family members and friends, Congressman Ryan notified Jim that he was coming down on a fact-finding mission. He traveled with members of the media, with some of these same family members, and with some members of the Concerned Relatives.

The Ryan party arrived in Guyana on November 16. Congressman Ryan and several of his group came over the back fence of our house at Lamaha Gardens in Georgetown. He introduced himself and shook hands all around. I had heard his name discussed in passing, but knew nothing else about him. He was friendly and asked how we were doing. Sharon Amos joined the group and told Ryan that he was invited only into Jonestown the next day, not to the Lamaha Gardens' house that evening. She asked him to leave. After a few minutes of carefully observing us to see if we were being coerced or held against our will, he left. He seemed to see and understand that we were excited about our Guyana mission.

In retrospect, I have more insight into why I was sent into Georgetown. Jim was never a fool. He wouldn't have assigned a person who was negative about Jonestown to live in Georgetown, especially since he knew about Congressman Ryan's impending trip. In addition, he wouldn't have sent someone who rebelled at his instructions. He must have seen me as appropriately enthusiastic about the Jonestown Agricultural Project. By that time, he had made his final plans and he knew what was in store for the community in Jonestown. He would have wanted someone who would follow Sharon Amos' directions if it came down to it.

There were many in Georgetown and Jonestown who loved it, so there were many others besides me whom Jim could have chosen. I have always felt that about fifty people would have gladly left Jonestown, given the opportunity. About ten more should have been sent out of Jonestown because they didn't deserve to live there and they took a lot of our time and energy. The rest of us would have wanted to continue the community, without Jim. When Ryan came in to the Georgetown house and asked me, I was absolutely honest when I told him that I loved it there.

The next day Congressman Ryan arrived in Jonestown, after a number of attempts all along the way to discourage him. Jonestown was prepared for Ryan's visit and the welcome was elaborate. The family talent show was awesome and enthusiastic. At one point, he spoke to the entire group assembled in the pavilion. He told everyone, amid cheers, that obviously many members loved it there and had created a dynamic community. He and his staff interviewed specific members and also others in the community. The evening ended on a very upbeat note. The community was at its best.

That evening, one resident tried to hand a note about leaving to a member of Ryan's entourage. Others were afraid to publicly announce their intentions, but did want out. In the morning, more people made contact with Ryan and other visitors. Ryan began making plans to leave with all of them. He had to arrange an additional plane to come and pick up the overflow at the Kaituma airport because more members wanted to leave. As families were separated, some members wanting to go, and some wanting to stay, it became a very tense and poignant time.

A fast-paced torrential rain fell and briefly delayed the departure, but finally, the trucks and trailers pulled out of Jonestown. Congressman Ryan, his following of staff and media, and the defectors all started out to the Port Kaituma airstrip about an hour away. At the airstrip, the first calamity of the day took place. Ryan and the others were waiting for the additional plane. A Jonestown truck with trailer drove up onto the airstrip. Men jumped out with guns and attacked the group. Congressman Ryan was shot and killed, as was Patty Parks, a long-time Temple member. Two innocent members of the media were also killed. Others, including Ryan aide Jackie Speier and Temple defectors Monica Bagby and Vern Gosney, were wounded. After that, the men boarded the truck and returned to Jonestown. The airstrip was littered with bodies of the killed and wounded. Everyone who was able ran into the jungle.

Back in Jonestown, Jim had called everyone to the Pavilion. He left the tape recorder on, recording his final message. After listening to the tape and speaking with the survivors who were still in Jonestown, and from watching Jim for the months before, I feel that I know what happened after that. He explained that the planes would be shot from the sky and that there was no way to keep going with the thriving community in Jonestown. He presented no other options. Soon the military would come in to take everyone back to the United States. There, members would face the charges of the congressman's death. He also reminded people what kinds of lives they had willingly left in the first place, and repeated his most frequently used mantra that things had only gotten worse.

Jim preached on and on about how there were no options left, other than "revolutionary suicide." He always spoke of revolutionary suicide as being the highest calling, dying for the principle you lived by. Only one woman stood and argued–Christine Miller. And she was such an asset in helping our community grow to be the best it could be.

But Jim was not to be dissuaded. He was tortured by the defections and the personal betrayals, and could anticipate but not tolerate the consequences he faced individually. He had spent several months, at least, concocting the plan and ordering, shipping, and storing the cyanide that he would use on this day. He had either planned for the exact happenstance, or had considered it a likely ending, so he was prepared for it. And by the end of the evening, he was able to persuade, coerce, and bully members to give the poison to the children and then drink the poisonous drink themselves. Only Jim and his nurse Annie Moore died from gunshots, and Annie died by her own hand. Everyone else had drunk the poison. These were the loyal people who had loved it in Jonestown and who had chosen not to leave. They were the visionaries who wanted Jonestown to thrive. Jim was unchallenged in his insanity and he could no longer make sense of his world. And he wouldn't let the others live without him. He felt HE was Jonestown. He did not want it to succeed without him or to even continue without him. He couldn't let go of it.

Before the final deaths in Jonestown, Jim sent a pre-arranged message to the house in Georgetown and the Temples in San Francisco and Los Angeles. The coded message let individuals in those locations know that people in Jonestown were dying. The pre-arranged instruction was for everyone at those locations to also take their lives. After that, the radio went quiet.

In Georgetown, I am sure that Sharon Amos was kept informed about what was transpiring in Jonestown. However, most of the rest of us in the house in Georgetown were not in the loop. We just went about our business as usual. I spent my day shopping, procuring, and placing and picking up orders. When I got back to the house at about five p.m., Sharon sent me out to bring the basketball team back from practice immediately. I was used to Sharon being very anxious, so I don't remember particularly noticing anything being more charged than usual for her. I went across town, and ran across a field to tell Stephan Jones, Lee Ingram and others that they needed to go back to the Georgetown house. We got home about six. About twenty members of the Guyanese Defense Force (GDF) were at the Lamaha Gardens house. They said that they had heard rumors about something going on in Jonestown, and they were stopping in to see that everything was all right with us. At that point, only Sharon knew any different, so the rest of us assured them that we were fine. They left about 6:30 p.m.

Stephan, Sharon and some others met privately. I found out later that, beginning at that very moment, Stephan began calling the San Francisco Temple and any other number where Temple members stateside might have gotten Jim's message. He called every half hour to tell them to stop ANY kind of parallel action. Everything was over – don't do ANYTHING. He never let up until he was sure that any thoughts of listening to Jim's instructions about joining the rest of our family in death had been stopped.

Most of the rest of the 50 or so in the house then walked to a Peoples National Congress talent show a few blocks away. We were oblivious to these discussions. When we came back, thirty GDF members were back at the Lamaha Gardens house. They had us all come into the living room and sit in a circle around the wall.

As we sat and waited, they brought out four body bags from the back of the house, from the area referred to as "Jim's apartment" or "room." We found out that it was Sharon and her three beautiful children, Liane, Martin and Christa. She had killed her family and then herself.

That was the first most of us knew about any of the tragedy of November 18. The police questioned us, asked our names, and ages. It was slow going, so finally, I stood up and went around the room, telling the names of everyone there.

We scattered around the house, with the Guyanese Defense Force monitoring our moves. The soldiers were young, seventeen to eighteen-year-old, kids who had no idea what they were doing there. We weren't told anything directly, as I recall, other than they were protecting us from ourselves. I don't know if we knew what that meant. Then the reports started coming in from Jonestown. First, we heard that there were 300 bodies of people who had died. The numbers kept changing, and the reports were more graphic and devastating. Mary Anne Casanova and I had worked on medical records, and we tried to figure out who might be living and who died. We kept hoping that a lot of people had survived somehow. We heard some of the names of folks trying to leave Jonestown, and who was shot at the airstrip, but most of the news from the radio was very spotty. We were in total denial that everyone in Jonestown, including several of Mary Anne's children, could be dead. So, we continued to try to paste together who might have survived.

I came up with a list of those I thought had survived. I sent the list to attorney Charles Garry, the Temple lawyer who had been rescued from Jonestown. Charles had been one of my heroes for many years. He had been one of Huey Newton's attorneys and an attorney for the Chicago Seven. He had always defended people of character. I got to know him fairly well, as I often picked him up at the airport in Georgetown and transported him around. I was sorry that he had gotten into the mess that was Peoples Temple right then. But he had been in Jonestown during Ryan's visit, and had been allowed to leave. Either Jim intended for him to leave, along with Mark Lane who was another attorney for the Temple at that time, or they did talk their way out of Jonestown. I'm not sure. A few days after November 18, Charles Garry seemed to be one who was communicating with family members and the media in San Francisco. He must have been in transit back to the United States by that time. I can't be sure because in the house, we got no newspaper, and we had no TV.

We listened to the radio and got what news we could glean from those sources. We also started calling our families and that is how we found out most of the information. The local Guyanese news had a news blackout, but international press could get the story from the Guyanese and print it in their own countries and internationally. Guyana didn't have any way to cope with what was going on, so just shut down any public discussion to figure out what role, if any, the Guyanese government played in the tragedy. During these first few days, I found out later, some of the survivors from the Georgetown house had been asked to return to Jonestown to try to identify bodies. It must have been too horrific for words. I was overwrought, so I'm sure no one even considered involving me in that. I can't imagine that additional trauma. We stayed in the house for another week or so.

Concerned Relatives, from California, had come down to support Congressman Ryan's investigative trip. Many in Concerned Relatives were former Peoples Temple members, and most had family members in Jonestown. Some had even gone into Jonestown with Ryan, and had visited with their relatives to be sure they were safe and happy. Once we were isolated in the Georgetown house, and surrounded by the Guyanese Defense Force soldiers, we saw some from the group across the field from the house, and even waved. They were probably hoping that their loved ones had somehow survived by being in Georgetown instead of being in Jonestown on November 18. Few of their loved ones survived. No one was allowed to enter or leave, without GDF permission.

Although there were small pockets of Temple folks around town, we were all kept separate. Tim Carter, Mike Carter, and Mike Prokes had walked out of Jonestown with suitcases of assets to be donated to the Soviet Union. They were secreted in one location. One person in the Lamaha Gardens house was arrested for assisting Sharon Amos in her murder/suicide. The large group who walked out of Jonestown in the morning of November 18 to go on a "picnic" was held at a different location, as was the Stoen family, Concerned Relatives, and Claire Janaro who had flown into Guyana that day. No one had an overview of who might be dangerous to someone else.

In the house, we vegetated. We talked, cried, formed alliances, found tiny things to keep us busy, dyed our underwear, adopted a local mange-covered dog that we nursed back to health, and spaced out. We spoke with our relatives back home frequently. I spoke with my mother, sister, and with my father. I learned later that once my father knew me to be alive, he went into his bedroom and stayed there for several days. The situation for all concerned was too tragic to deal with.

No one knew what would happen next. After a week or so, we were told that all the women and some of the older men of the house (with a few exceptions) were going back to the US. One of the survivors, Nedra Yates, decided to stay and marry the GDF man she had met while he was on duty in the Lamaha Garden house.

The basketball team had to wait until there were enough U.S. air marshals so that each basketball player had his own escort on the flight from Guyana back to New York. By then, the rumor was that the basketball team was also the "hit" squad and that the hit squad would kill targeted enemies of the Temple. I'm not sure where the rumor started but you could look at us there in the house and know that was absurd. We were devastated. For another thing, the basketball team contained youth that had no desire to be violent – they just wanted to play basketball and compete in a national Guyanese basketball championship game. Since the team was made up of our best basketball players, of course they were young, strong, tall, and energetic. But, they too had just lost their families and their community in Jonestown.

I had coupled up with one of the men staying in Guyana, so I decided to stay and wait until the others went back. I was not happy about returning to the US. I had fallen in love with Guyana. About twenty of us stayed in Georgetown, while the other thirty-five returned to the United States. We stayed briefly at the Lamaha Garden house, and then moved into a hotel in town. We were monitored during that time, with soldiers in the house or nearby. We stayed in a hotel for about a week. In early December, when they had sufficient air marshals to escort us individually, the U.S. government flew us from Georgetown to Kennedy Airport in New York City.

About eight Peoples Temple members stayed on in Georgetown for various reasons. Some were signatories on Peoples Temple bank accounts and documents. Others had some involvement with the ongoing investigation about the events in Jonestown, at the airstrip, or at the Georgetown house. At this time, the Guyanese and the US governments were both looking for a scapegoat to charge with some connection with the deaths. It couldn't just be dropped without an arrest or finding blame. So the governments tried to investigate who might be charged. That group stayed several more months before being allowed to leave Guyana.

The rest of us left Guyana as soon as the air marshals were available. I can remember that at the Georgetown airport, we all emptied our pockets of any Guyanese money, and gave it to the Peoples Temple folks remaining in Guyana. The currency was not traded internationally, and would do us no good in the US. However, upon arrival in the US, that meant that we were all literally penniless. That just added to our depression and sense of loss. We were returning, under duress, to a place we had hoped to leave behind permanently.

CHAPTER 9
Leaving My Home in Guyana

We flew from Georgetown to New York's Kennedy Airport, under guard. After all non-Peoples Temple passengers deplaned, we were each escorted out to our very own bus (two Peoples Temple members and at least two marshals per bus). Then we were taken to large Winnebago campers where we were each held separately and interrogated. We were kept there for about 14 hours. I remember at some point being given some McDonald's fast food. It dropped like lead in my stomach, after having had fresh, tasty food for so long. The interrogators tried the good cop-bad cop routine, and everything else. They would leave me alone, and then come back and say that someone told them that I knew everything. They asked me some specific names of people who had been in Jonestown. I found out later that they had asked about the armed people who had supposedly gone to the airport in the truck. I hadn't pieced together exactly what had happened on the 18th – since the house in Georgetown was monitored, and since we had no direct knowledge of what had happened – and it still wasn't clear to me. Also I wasn't coping well with what I did know, so expecting anything else was out of the question.

When they started asking me about my personal situation, I asked for a lawyer and refused to speak to them any more. My mother had come to Kennedy Airport and was insisting on seeing me, and on getting me a lawyer, but they totally disregarded anything she asked, along with requests of parents and family members of other returnees.

They had their own agenda and answered to no one. Eventually, we were released from the trailers and went into the airport. That's when a number of us received subpoenas to appear before the San Francisco Grand Jury, which had convened to investigate a possible conspiracy in the murder of Congressman Ryan.

Later, I heard that Attorney William Kunstler was watching the situation and would be available if we wanted to file a class-action lawsuit claiming that our civil rights were violated. Our civil rights undoubtedly were violated. Most of us were just barely surviving and just couldn't take that one on.

The U.S. government housed us in a New York City motel one night, and then flew us to San Francisco. I flew to San Francisco since I wanted to be surrounded by my adopted Peoples Temple family. I remember I arrived at the San Francisco Airport, and a newspaper reporter asked me how I felt about being "home." I frankly told him that my home was in Guyana, and that I'd had to leave my "home" to be here. My good friends picked me up from the airport, and we went back to the Temple on Geary and Fillmore Streets.

A lot of the file workers and secretaries did not get to go to Guyana because many essentials, like clothing, personal items, building materials, equipment and food, were still purchased here and sent down to Jonestown to stock the developing community. It took superb organization and commitment of those skilled in those areas. In San Francisco and all over California, there was a frenzy of activity to collect and send basics to the nearly one thousand residents in Guyana. Some members who stayed in the United States had assignments to work on public relations and fundraising. Others had skills necessary to help get people packed and ready. Since their skills were still needed in the United States, they stayed here. These were the people I returned to.

A California State Judge appointed Attorney Robert Fabian in San Francisco to oversee the finances. Peoples Temple had incurred debts in bringing back the bodies from Jonestown as well as many other expenses. One decision Fabian made was to evacuate us from the Temple building on Geary Boulevard in about February 1979 so that it could be sold for the money due the government. The ten of us still living there moved into several different Peoples Temple communes throughout the city. I made one or two trips to Washington, D.C. to see my mom, but couldn't be comfortable with so much free time. I was a wreck. We survivors felt totally isolated and could only find comfort with others who could understand our common trauma. We weren't communicating our needs then, but were just barely surviving.

I got a job within a few days of returning to San Francisco. I was distraught but also angry. The US government had taken my passport in exchange for my "debt" to them for my airfare back from Guyana. I just knew I had to pay that off right then. I felt that they had no right to hold my passport in the first place, and I decided to get it back. I got a job through Kelly Services and immediately paid off my debt to the government and got my passport back. That was good therapy for me. Also I could then send money to one of the members being held in the Guyanese jail, give money to some of the other returnees who had no income yet, and not feel so powerless. As soon as I went to work, I never missed a day. Work was far easier than facing idle time at home.

I was assigned a court-appointed attorney, George Walker, to represent me at the grand jury proceedings. When I went to meet with him, my sister Linda went along. He was curious about her – in case she was there to monitor what I said. We both assured him that she was not in Peoples Temple, and she was my protector at this point. After our discussion, we both agreed that taking the Fifth Amendment was the best option. The grand jury was on a fishing expedition, and was trying to find someone – anyone—to place blame on. In spite of really tough questioning, I took the Fifth Amendment throughout, and left the room a sobbing mess. Some of those who had been subpoenaed did speak freely. None of us was charged.

Many of us continued to live in communes with other Peoples Temple members for about the first year. Former members living throughout the Bay Area would gather together from time to time, thinking that we "should," but we weren't much help to each other. Some were able to move on with their lives more easily than others. Some got married and/or had children right away. I felt that my last several years in Guyana had made my transition harder because I had to reestablish myself here in the US. I had been very close to my friends and the events in Guyana, and my thoughts frequently went back to them. But, I finally realized that each of us had suffered the most we could have suffered and still survive. My details might be different, but we had all lost too much to get caught up in who lost more, or who was the most traumatized. Living in pure Peoples Temple communes was workable for about a year.

Those were very tough days. Almost every day brought some new story, finding, suicide, tragedy or headline associated with Peoples Temple. Just when we had put on a stoic face, everything would blow up again. I remember crying many times over my typewriter on my job. I never told anyone on the job anything about my past. I tried to stay busy, kept my job, started going to school at night at Golden Gate University and then San Francisco State, tried to find a Peoples Temple boyfriend who could give some comfort, and tried to work – but those were tough days. I had not even made a positive decision that I wanted to live.

I have been asked many times if I consider the deaths in Jonestown and four in Georgetown as murder or suicide. After reflecting on this now for many years, I feel like I know my truth. Undoubtedly, all the children and those who had limited understanding of Jim and of what was going on during the last days in Jonestown were murdered. They were not able to choose. For those adults who wanted to leave and were not permitted to, they too were murdered. Only two people in Jonestown were shot, Jim Jones, and his nurse and my friend, Annie Moore. The other six hundred who died in Jonestown chose to commit suicide rather than return to their old lives in the United States. Did they have full knowledge of what was happening outside of Jonestown and Guyana? No. Was their reality scripted and distorted by Jim? Yes. Did they want to come back to the United States and live as they had been living before? No.

Many people had felt that Jonestown was their paradise. Jim didn't leave it at that. Day after day, he would give tirades over the loudspeaker about the desperate situation for people of color in the United States. I too would not have chosen to come back. I loved Jonestown. I didn't want to leave it.

I came back from Guyana with a wonderful trunk, which was 4'x3'x3', and it was about one-fourth filled. I had left some things in Jonestown since I was only going to Georgetown for a few weeks – but had very little anyway. We all had our belongings in these heavy plywood trunks. When I got back to the United States, everything at all related to Peoples Temple that came my way would go into the trunk. It took me twenty-seven years to go back and sort through what I collected over those first years. I just couldn't deal with it before then.

For my survival, there were two major hurdles for me to overcome. The first was that my memories of the previous eight years all included folks who were now dead. The second hurdle was filling my time with activities and gauze so that I wouldn't have a minute to re-live the trauma. I just had to stay busy, just as I had stayed busy in the Temple. It couldn't be just busy-work. I wasn't interested in visiting malls or watching mindless television programs. I wanted a meaningful way to use my time. I wanted to continue to make the world a better place.

With my recollections of the immediate eight years before November 18, the pictures and experiences would haunt me at night. I had nothing to fill my days and nights – so many hours to fill. That was a further reason for me not to drink or use drugs, too, because then I couldn't control what I would think about. As with all tragedies and trauma, only time lessens that horror, and there was no way to speed that process along.

All of us handled the tragedy in one similar way. We just stopped our retrieval systems from pulling up names of people in Peoples Temple and people lost. I'd see a person with a familiar personality type or prototype, and rather than trying to pull up the name, I'd just stop there. I couldn't remember who had lived or died. I couldn't remember who had or hadn't been in Guyana. I could only remember the people's faces.

One evening, my friend Jim R. from Peoples Temple, who had worked at the Welfare Department with me, and I sat at a Vietnamese restaurant in Potrero Hill in San Francisco. A woman came into this restaurant. I glanced up and just knew that I knew her – but couldn't recall who she was. I told Jim, who discounted it. I insisted I knew her, but that was all I knew. She came over to the table, and greeted us. I had worked with her for seven years. She had a desk next to me. For a minute, I gave her a very blank stare, and then had some vague memory. I was so traumatized that my only way to survive was to shut the door on those faces and experiences. She re-introduced herself as Carole Shirrell. I was happy she came over though I am sure I didn't show it.

I found Carole had passed on to my former co-workers that she had seen me, because soon after that, I got a wonderful letter from two kids I had known from that time at the welfare department. I had worked with their mother when they were young, and they came into the office often. They wrote to tell me how happy they were that I survived. They were very sweet and thoughtful. If I had been in my right mind, I would have immediately written back to them and thanked them. I didn't have a chance to write to them. I also wasn't that sure that I was happy about my own survival.

The City of San Francisco set up some re-entry programs for the survivors. There was counseling available and some other support systems too. Dr. Chris Hatcher, who turned out to be a jewel for many of the survivors, was one of the counselors. He later attended the yearly memorial ceremonies in Oakland and established a strong bond with many of us, but I wasn't in a trusting mood then, so I didn't take advantage of that. Some of the survivors did. I later found out that Chris Hatcher was a terrific ally, and talking to him might have made the transition a little easier. Years later, I wrote him a long letter and then tried to find him, to send it to him. It was returned several times, so finally I destroyed the letter – it had too much honesty to let it just hang around. He died soon after I had sort of regrouped and was looking around for my oldest Temple friends again, around the time of the twentieth anniversary. I'm sorry I didn't meet him.

Time actually tested my desire to live. I had been booked for all my waking hours for so long that time became my worst enemy. I couldn't be idle. I couldn't find peace in relaxation. I worked eight to five every day. But then, I'd have evenings and weekends to contend with. I took computer classes for the most part – moving away from the social work and human contact aspect of my work experience. I didn't want and couldn't cope with emotional attachments on the job. I wanted to face a computer and interact with it, crying or not. After that, sometimes, I could do homework and fill up a few more hours.

That left Friday night and the weekend – my hardest time. That is when all of us would get the most depressed – too much time on our hands. Nothing frivolous seemed to help – shopping, partying, drinking, or spending money, just reminded me that I didn't have a greater cause to be working for. I dated several Temple men over that year, but I was a basket case, and none of the relationships worked out.

Looking back, that might have saved me from the AIDS epidemic. I only dated Temple guys who had been celibate, like me, or who had only had sex within the Temple so had not spread the disease. That was indeed a miracle. One other good friend in the Temple went through a period of having multiple partners, and she did die of AIDS. If AIDS had come along in the late 1960s instead of late 1970s, I would not have survived it, I am sure. At one point, I was dating several Peoples Temple survivors. One put his foot down and said that I should make up my mind which person I wanted to date, and stop flitting around. That was very good advice. I made my choice – him—and it lasted for about a year.

I had a close call in San Francisco around that time. I was attending Golden Gate University and I had borrowed Linda's car to drive to class because it was scary coming home at night by bus from the downtown campus. I had driven about three blocks from her house and I stopped at a light or stop sign. As I sat there, a man ran up to my car, yanked open the door, and tried to pull me out of the car. There was no one around for a few minutes. I had my seatbelt on, and he couldn't pull me out. I honked my horn and screamed. Finally, another car came over the hill behind me and he ran off. I felt that the seatbelt had certainly saved my life that time. I reported it to the police and, I think they watched that corner for other attempted car-jackings. I actually wasn't sure what was going to happen. A carjacking would have been the best of the scenarios I thought about. That was yet another near miss in my life. Even though my life was difficult, I certainly fought him off as if I wanted to live!

In early 1980, Bunny Mann, the former Guyanese Ambassador came to San Francisco. He had dated Paula Adams for years while she was in Guyana. She was part of the Guyana leadership team, but not exactly one of Jim's personal secretaries. She was a wonderfully creative and insightful friend of mine, especially in Guyana. Bunny had looked us up, since he had come to know some of us. I asked him for Paula's address because I was anxious to contact her, and he refused. I had known him for several years by that point. He had always been a jerk, but I was especially angry that he would take the time to contact other Peoples Temple folks, and then not allow us to communicate with her.

A short time after his visit, he killed Paula, their child, and himself. I was very sorry to find that out.

My grief would wash over me in waves. Sometimes a news story would trigger it, sometimes a person I saw, and sometimes nothing. I was alive but not committed to life. I was way beyond needing a brief therapy appointment once or twice a week. I was drowning in guilt and failure. I looked around for help I could use.

CHAPTER 10
Another Community Steps In-Synanon

Charles Dederich was a feisty and ingenious founder of Synanon, the residential drug-treatment organization that grew into thousands of members. Tens of thousands of drug addicts and alcoholics came through its doors and were cleaned up and rehabilitated, beginning in the late 1950s. There was no other organization like it then, and many of the drug rehabilitation programs existing now are offshoots of Synanon, started by former members. The foundation was based on these tenets: No violence, no threat of violence, aerobic exercise five times a week, and the Synanon Game.

About half of the membership had come in as drug addicts and the other half came in because they wanted to help change the lives of the drug addicts, and live with a vibrant group of people in a close-knit community. From the beginning, people did not come to Synanon to get rich, but it was a rich community. You had your own job, and other people had jobs that would take care of your other basic needs. You would work in the school, or in the advertising office, and someone else would work in the kitchen, or the laundry, or the automotive shop. There were many departments where you could work, or learn a new skill. You were expected to do a great job. Cooks prepared and served all meals in the large kitchen and dining room. Another crew cleaned up after the meals. A fleet of cars was available for you to pick one and go out for the day. Mechanics kept them in good condition. Many members had their own motorcycles that they maintained or had help in maintaining. Everything was included in the lifestyle. You could play bridge or poker around the pool in the summer, while watching the Olympics, or a movie, or some other sport. You didn't get a lot of money, but you lived a lifestyle that money couldn't buy you. The best dentist and doctors I've ever been treated by lived there. People from every race and socio-economic level lived in Synanon and everything was integrated. There was a dynamism that made every day fun and unique. Synanon was a social, not a political, experiment. Those who moved in wanted to live in an integrated and satisfying environment. We provided an alternate lifestyle for drug addicts who had to find a new manner of living.

Synanon worked because of the magic created in the "Synanon Game." The Game was a circular setting where there was open, loud, outrageously funny, and hostile communication. No one was above being "gamed." Synanon used this setting to handle all issues of living and working in community. The Game was the great leveler. Everyone was equal in the Game, and could say anything to anyone. Just as there is a saying now of, "What happens in Las Vegas stays in Las Vegas," our saying was "what happens in a Synanon Game stays there." You didn't discuss a Game with anyone outside the Game. At times, there were issues brought up in a Game that an Elder (a long-time Synanon member) might follow up on – but not in a gossipy manner. If a person's boss was rude or disrespectful, a person could yell, scream, talk, name-call, or whatever – in the Game.

All kinds of issues were dealt with in the circle. Former drug addicts were held accountable for their behavior and their work effort. They were expected to enter into a civilized community and behave properly, even if they didn't know what that meant. They learned how to become clean, sober, and hard-working citizens. There were high expectations that the new members would allow the community to be tranquil and well run. Then, in the Game, all other issues would be aired and discussed. Early on in its history, the only type of Synanon Game was loud, boisterous, and verbally combative. Many members had been in prison or jail, and it was necessary to get their full attention in the Game. They were re-educated and re-directed into finding challenge and satisfaction in wholesome activities.

Betty Coleman Dederich was a former heroin addict who had

cleaned up in Synanon. She then went on to marry Chuck. She was the mother that many people were looking for – she chastised you and loved you; she was tough or soft – as you needed. She was a giant of a leader in Synanon and was a wonderful contrast to Chuck, who was more of a hard-liner. She even had a Synanon Game named after her because she was intuitive and insightful. She knew that the same type of Game just couldn't be played with every person or even the same person, all the time. "Betty's Game" was for people who had lost a loved one, or had an illness, or who needed support through some event. They would be in a setting more like a listening or confiding Game. The Game could give comfort as well as confrontation. Most Games had both types of gaming during the evening. Former drug addicts could see how it was possible to work out solutions to problems. Everyone was impressed at resolutions reached in Games. By just talking through things thoroughly, we could look at things more evenly and get to know each other more intimately. Former drug addicts might need a "straightening out" kind of Game a lot of the time. Over time, once they had more insight, they could make use of either type of Game and participate and talk to others in either one.

An extension of the Synanon Game was the Synanon Trip. This was a several-day experience that was used to make people more intimate and more sensitive to others. It was built along the lines of "encounter group" sessions, but with different activities – learning sessions, gaming, discussions, introspection, exercise, and communication. Those who participated were the "trippers," and they didn't get much sleep as defenses were broken down, and new bonds were formed. The people orchestrating the event were long-time Synanon members, particularly those who had the confidence of other members because of their judgment and wisdom. They were called "Wizards." The "trippers" were isolated from others in the community, kept off of their jobs, and just led through the events that had been planned. The purpose was to help them form new friendships and get to know themselves better. The yearly "Trips" were special events, mostly for newer members or members who had gone through a recent tragedy. The sleep deprivation and gaming guaranteed more intimate friendships.

One of the most famous Synanon events was the "bald heads." In Tomales Bay, Synanon constructed a huge new kitchen and food storage facility. Upstairs, the architect had mistakenly left a beam across the ceiling at about five feet off the ground. Everyone who saw it laughed about it. They finally decided to put some sort of bunting around it so that no one would get hurt when they inevitably walked into it. When Chuck walked through to inspect the building and saw the "Beam," he was furious. He had a Synanon Game and told all who had built the building, leaving the "Beam," to go shave their heads. The architects did shave their heads. Over the next few days, with more gaming, others realized they too were culpable. Their wives shaved their heads, and the other workers shaved theirs. By the time it was over, there were many bald heads. Some people kept their heads bald for some time after that.

Synanon wasn't all talk. Several times over the years, Synanon got in trouble with people outside of the community. "No violence or threat of violence" was practiced inside but not outside of Synanon. When occasionally people would trespass onto Synanon property, they would be physically assaulted and tossed off. Once, when some of the kids were riding bikes on the mountainous roads of Badger, some people drove by and yelled names at them. The Synanon men went after the cars, brought the drivers back on to the property, and shaved their heads.

Another time, an attorney was taking a good look at Synanon, and someone put a rattlesnake in his mailbox. Chuck and two others were charged with conspiracy and the two Synanon members were found guilty, and served jail sentences.

When Betty died of cancer in the mid-1970s, Chuck started drinking once more. From that time on, his moods and his leadership were unreliable. Other Synanon leadership emerged and ran the organization, with Chuck as a figurehead and a good friend, but not in control of any of the major decisions. He had come down off of his pedestal and people had a healthier perspective of him, that he was human, after all.

In the mid-1970s, while Peoples Temple was looking around for ways to outfit folks in Guyana and in the Temples in California, we made our first contact with Synanon. Synanon was thriving. It was supported by non-governmental sources, cash and material donations, sales of advertising products, and cheap labor of the members of the community. Since Synanon was a non-profit, it could solicit donations of many items, including clothing and food. Peoples Temple started getting donations of clothing and supplies from Synanon—one non-profit organization to another. We received shoes, clothes, machinery, food, and other things over the years. These supplies were sent down to Guyana, especially after 1976.

The people from Peoples Temple and from Synanon developed friendships and mutual understanding, since both residential communities were fully integrated, and idealistic, and built around a communal message. Strong, courageous, and entertaining leaders, who were both brilliant and dysfunctional, had started both groups. In addition, both groups encouraged or required strong commitment and loyalty to the leader and the program. Many members of Synanon understood too well about the pressure of a group on each individual. They hadn't had the exact experiences of those of us in Peoples Temple, but they came the closest of understanding the whole picture—how it was to live in a rich, exciting community, how individual needs might be secondary to group needs in a specific area, how things could get out of hand (just as they had in Synanon from time to time), how important the relationships were, how a leader could flounder, and what a loss it would be to lose it all.

There were some people in Synanon who had come to fear the ranting and bull-headedness of Chuck Dederich. After hearing Jim's final tape from Jonestown, and hearing what a madman he was, they were even more alarmed with Chuck. These feelings didn't seem to come as much from leadership as from the general population.

From my perspective, Chuck was egotistical and irascible, but he surrounded himself with other strong egos. Just like a bull challenges other bulls, Chuck would take on these others. He loved the exercise of quick thinking, quick wit and dynamic interchange. He would pursue any interchange until he could have the last word, though. But Chuck had others in top management who would not have been manipulated into death for any reason; they would have stopped it. The Synanon leadership was successful and well off. They had a bright future. They were not isolated in the far reaches of a South American rain forest. He had people in leadership who would never have let him get so far off track. Others did take the reins from Chuck when he got too heavily into drinking. Regardless, Synanon stepped right in to help us. In early 1979, Synanon was having a "Synanon Trip." Several San Francisco

Peoples Temple survivors had started visiting Synanon after November 18, 1978. They had developed friendships there and didn't have to start fresh to explain why they were distraught or overwhelmed. Synanon met us with open arms – even though there was some trepidation. Only three of us got involved with Synanon, and I was the only one who stayed on after a few months.

Those of us who have lived in communities have a brotherhood/sisterhood that binds us. When Mt. Carmel burned down, and when MOVE was destroyed in Philadelphia, I was shattered. I felt like my very same brothers and sisters had died, all over again. There is an undeniable bond between peoples who have taken a path away from the consumerism and gluttony that surrounds us.

I started going around Synanon just to play the Synanon Game. I kept coming for about six months, on Friday nights. I was spending time at Synanon on Friday nights and at some Sunday breakfasts. It started as a way to fill my weekends with activities.

In about September of 1979, two other survivors and I moved away from the Sutter Street commune and to Potrero Hill across the street from the SF Synanon House, an old paint factory. I started going over for Saturday work crews as well as Sunday brunch and other activities. I was beginning to develop friendships through the Synanon Game. Spending time with only Peoples Temple members was not working out for me. I was certainly needy, and everyone else was just trying to cope, too. It was such a difficult time for everyone. I think it was just too hard trying to keep a positive, upbeat, interesting bond when we were so stressed. I had to move outside of the group of Peoples Temple survivors.

A few of the guys from Synanon were interested in dating me. They came to Games with me, and walked me home. Eventually, I started dating a long-time Synanon resident. In January 1980, I applied to move into Synanon. For me, this meant that I didn't maintain my friendships with most Peoples Temple folks. It wasn't a Synanon rule, but I didn't multitask well at that point. I just had to be in one place, at one time, with a relatively small circle of friends. I also wanted friends who didn't depend on me to be coherent and positive all the time. It was too much pressure for me. I was walking and talking, but still very numb.

One night, before I was going over to a Synanon Game night, I had a drink. I drank very rarely. It might have been around the anniversary, in November. When I got to the Game, my Synanon boyfriend gamed me about drinking. One of the more sane members walked both of us through it. By then, they knew me well enough to know I wasn't an alcoholic, but that I had traumatic baggage I carried around. That was the power of the Synanon Game – you could hear the whole range of feelings, and find your own place there.

I actually loved to hear the Game played, and I especially loved the Game when someone actually "used the Game" to delve emotionally deeply into his or her feelings. That freed up the whole Game to go deeper and not be so superficial. In the Game, you didn't have to make sense. The Game was for you to say what you needed to say to move on. The Game in fact was my salvation. I do believe in geographical cures, which is how Synanon worked so well as drug rehabilitation. It pulled you out of the environment where you had been making poor choices, and gave you responsibilities. It expected the best, protected you from peer pressure, and showed you how to have fun a different way. It re-taught me healthy survival skills and gave power to my inner voice. It taught me to listen to me, to be honest with myself always. In the Game, you find that you are not as perfect as you'd like to think, and that there are many others in the same boat. And, you find that talking about it makes you all much better friends, at a more authentic level of friendship.

My Temple friends and my family all thought I was crazy because I moved into another cult. I'm sure my mother was the most distraught because she had seen me from day one, when I returned from Guyana. But, I don't remember her trying to talk me out of it. I felt that the survival muscle had kicked in for me and that if I wanted to live and have a decent life, I had to begin in a safe, nurturing, busy environment with some people who understood me a bit. So, on my own, without any encouragement from anyone outside of Synanon, I moved in to the San Francisco Synanon house at Oyster Point. After I finished my semesters of computer classes, I moved up to the Synanon offices and properties in Tomales Bay, and started working in the Synanon data processing office as a computer operator. I didn't even see it as a choice. I felt like I had to do it if I wanted to survive.

For the first few years at Synanon, my only Peoples Temple contacts were with Larry Layton while he was in San Francisco jail, and I went down to San Francisco by bus many weekends. Larry had been arrested and was awaiting trial for Jonestown-related charges. I usually went with a good friend, Leticia. She had moved into Synanon as a battered wife, and we had a great friendship. We spoke Spanish all the time and I loved it. She didn't speak English very well. We did our Synanon-required aerobics, running twenty minutes four times a week, together and bitched the whole time. I remember, on one public bus trip into San Francisco, we spoke about private things in Spanish all the way down. When we arrived, someone on the bus who looked like a gringo turned and spoke to us in Spanish. We were actually dismayed and surprised. But we had a big laugh later.

At the jail, I would go through all the security to see Larry. It was hard. I knew they were monitoring everything we said, so I didn't really discuss what was going on with me – what Synanon was like, about my love-matches. I just went to offer solidarity to Larry. Many of us survivors felt that we could easily have ended up in prison as the government looked for someone to be held accountable. When Larry got out briefly, before sentencing, I felt he was in good stead with his family, and I immersed myself in Synanon. I kept infrequent contact with my friend, Laurie Efrein, via letters. I was like an ostrich with my head in the sand for several years.

One of my wisest friends in Synanon was Wilbur Beckham. He was an Elder, and Betty Dederich's brother. Once, he told me he loved sitting at meals with me because our conversation could take us all around the world. It struck home with me because I always did consider myself a citizen of the world. Synanon addressed the details of life – to "debug" life. I like those details worked out, too. But I wanted to view the panorama of life. I was nurtured while I was in Synanon but I always felt that my radical political opinions were just sitting on a shelf, waiting to be awakened again.

I worked in Synanon's data processing department for three years, made good friends, and had a setting to vent my deepest feelings regularly. At first, I only cried and blubbered in the Games. I was happiest listening to other people talk about their own problems – I just needed to see that the world was still going on all around me, and that when I was ready to step onto the pathway, I would have help. I did ok on my job, since it kept me busy. I taught word-processing and data file management, as well as doing backups on the computers. I had worked as a secretary in the MIS branch of a company for a year when I returned to San Francisco and had gone to classes in programming and file management. The work was exactly what I wanted – some time in conversation and teaching class, and some time by myself just massaging the machines to do backups. Perfect for me, and I had great friends in that department.

I worked on the cube – which was working for seven straight days, long hours, and then having seven days off. Groups of us rode motorcycles all around California during our free time. I tried being a motorcycle driver myself, but flipped over on my bike when I was riding and decided that I'd just be a passenger from then on.

I was "Love-matched" to my first Synanon boyfriend, Jerry, in the spring of 1980. This was a Synanon ceremony likened to a church marriage. It wasn't a civil ceremony, but it was considered "marriage" in Synanon. Synanon was a monogamous community, with about the same numbers of members unfaithful as in the larger community. We stayed together for two years. He was truly good at nurturing, and taking care of a despondent, crying, emotional partner. That was definitely me for the about the first two and a half years after I returned. But then I was ready, finally, to move on. I didn't want to be a victim anymore. But he didn't want an equal partner. We separated in the spring of 1982. I was more able to take charge of my life. I still hurt, and still used my Synanon Game to clear out the tears, but I had made progress.

CHAPTER 11
Placing One Foot in Front of the Other

I started dating Ron, my husband, that spring. He is Puerto Rican, and speaks fluent Spanish and English, in addition to a number of other qualities. Ron grew up in New York City. His brother, Bobby, started using heroin at about fourteen. In his late teens, he tried a "geographic cure" by moving into Synanon in California. Ron was Bobby's youngest sibling. They have a middle sister, Evelyn. Ron finished high school and joined the Navy, in the late 1960s. He was on an aircraft carrier and fortunately never got near Vietnam. He was stationed in the Mediterranean. When he got out of the Navy, many of his friends had overdosed or were in prison. He came out to visit his brother, who worked directly with Betty Dederich. Bobby moved out of Synanon when Betty Dederich died of cancer in the mid-1970s, but never used heroin again.

Ron truly liked Synanon and also saw no future for himself back in his old neighborhood, so he joined a small group of Synanon residents living in New York, and then moved out to California. Even after his brother moved out, Ron stayed because he loved the community, and all the activities, and thrived in the environment. He worked in automotive, at the gas station Synanon owned, in customer service for the advertising gifts and specialties department, in food service, and as a volunteer fireman.

I wasn't easy to be with then because I was still so traumatized by my experiences in Guyana, but I was getting better as time went on.

We were love-matched that summer. We did a lot of activities together. We hosted international dinners for the kids in the school, taped lots of TV shows for the Synanon media center (videos for residents to watch without commercials), traveled on long motorcycle rides all around the state, transported kids on outings, taxied people to airports, and did our jobs. If I am ever stuck on a desert island, I want Ron to be there with me. He is ingenious. He can make treasures out of junk. And that's good, because he does love to collect junk. Ron has lots of interests and loves thinking "outside the box." As soon as I was single, he started his pursuit of me. We've been together over 29 years!

Synanon never had the political aspect of Peoples Temple. Many of the residents were conservative or apolitical. In many ways, it was like Club Med. We were catered to. It was a very comfortable, clean, sober, safe, and monogamous community.

I learned a lot in Synanon and was cared for lovingly. Residents in Synanon got "WAM" or "Walking Around Money." It was based on time in Synanon. At one point, after I'd lived and worked in Synanon for over five years, I wrote a letter to the CEO and requested a raise. Those of us having between five and ten years in Synanon were each getting a monthly pittance. We'd get bonuses from time to time. But our monthly income was somewhere around thirty-five dollars. Everything was provided, food, housing, entertainment, and more. Nevertheless, I thought we needed a raise. I wrote kind of a "class-action" letter and included all of us who were in the same boat. The group included a terrific dentist, great artists and craftsmen, hard workers, and me. We got a raise. It was a great result of exercising my muscles. I was determined not to be passive in Synanon, or anywhere else. I wanted to keep my eyes forever open.

In 1983, I moved from Marin County down to work in the data processing department in Central California. We had two Synanon properties up in the hills near the Sequoia National Park in Badger. The Home Place was an elegant property where most of Synanon leadership, including Chuck Dederich and his new wife Ginny, lived in luxury. Eighty people lived there. About seven miles away, I lived on the second property called "The Strip" since the buildings were all placed in proximity to an airstrip. Earlier, Synanon owned and flew small airplanes onto the property and stored them in a huge shed. That ended before I moved into

Synanon. Two hundred or more of us lived on that property. It was lovely and utilitarian, but not as posh as the Home Place.

One job I volunteered to do in Synanon was supervise the kids overnight. After kids went to sleep, parents and members of the community would take shifts as "P.O.D." an acronym for "Parent on Duty." We would spend the night in the children's dorms as security. The kids were grouped by age and sex, and lived in dorms. Synanon hired "demonstrators" (Synanon residents) to supervise the daily lives of the kids. People who loved children were generally working in those positions. Parents would spend quality time with their kids when they could, but wouldn't focus on the daily rituals of waking, bathing, brushing teeth, and getting them ready for bed. I loved spending time with the kids at night, and doing the POD duty every couple of months. Spending time with children has always been an uplifting experience for me.

Synanon then had a vow of "childlessness." No one in Synanon was having children. In theory, it was to take care of the world's children. But, it meant there were no young children. The youngest – age seven or so – was rapidly getting older with no new, young children. I started gaming (playing the Synanon Game) about having a child, and being around children. A number of other couples had also started their own gaming about having children. I got a job change and worked in the Synanon School as a demonstrator.

The school was set up like the kibbutz in Israel. Some parents were spectacular, and some were dismal. Some kids loved the experience, and some hated it. Many of the kids have since told me that they missed having more contact with their parents. Others felt that their experiences were unique and rich. I worked as a demonstrator and as a teacher. My friends from Synanon who are in my life now all had kids in the Synanon School, or worked with the kids – Jane Davis, Sonja Eriksson, Lavonne Gaston, and Elena Broslovsky. As the kids got older, less staff was needed. At that time in Badger, all the kids (Synanon and others) living near Kings Canyon National Park attended a one-room public school house. The schoolroom was of multi-aged kids from the mountains, from Synanon, and from the Hare Krishna, who lived around us – and many of them worked for Synanon. The PTA meetings were certainly entertaining. When the kids moved away from Badger into Visalia and elsewhere, they were terrific students. They had their fundamental skills and were high achievers. Once the kids went off to school, we just needed a few staff members to supervise them. I moved on to another job in the accounts receivables branch of sales. Maybe because I had lived in community for so long with minimum income and no bills to pay, or maybe just because I wasn't good at Accounts Receivables, that job was a very bad fit for me.

I started working in the Law Office as a legal secretary and occasional translator. I taught English to the mostly Spanish-speaking workers who cooked our delicious food, and conversational Spanish to members.

In about 1985, in Badger, Ron and I decided we definitely wanted to have a child. We joined forces with the other couples in Synanon who also wanted to have children. The era of "childlessness" in Synanon was about to come to an end in spite of some disagreement from the top. Some of those who wanted kids were in leadership or were very successful sales people. All of us just went ahead making our plans. We united in the effort and it worked out for all of us. Ron and I decided I would try to become pregnant and we would begin the process for adopting a child at the same time.

At that time, in the middle of our personal adoption/artificial insemination activities, my legal secretary job with the Synanon Law Office ended. I started working in the dining room – cleaning tables, making coffee. Then Ron lost his job at Synanon because the job of customer service in sales was very exacting – too exacting for him. He was then hired by a connected business, Synanon Second Market. That group collected surplus supplies of food and equipment and shipped to locations needing that specific item. I thought the poor timing of those lay-offs was unforgivable. One Synanon administrator actually told us to postpone or cancel our adoption plans. How absurd. I started "Working Out," which means I worked off the property on a job teaching English as a Second Language at a business college in Visalia. Ron got a job teaching comedy traffic school, also in Visalia. We continued with our plans to have a child.

A group of six couples had moved ahead with having children. Several of the potential fathers had previously had vasectomies. A few of the fathers had vasectomy reversals. Other couples tried artificial insemination. My husband and I tried artificial insemination, beginning in 1987. We also started sending out some adoption resumes. We sent to all of the embassies in Central and South America, and every other place we could think of. I had always thought about adopting. After seeing and knowing Jim Jones' beautiful family, it made me even more excited by the prospect.

Another couple hired a law firm and adoption counselor to find a child for them to adopt. They paid a $500 retainer so the attorney would look for their child. The same attorney also collected adoption resumes of others, with no money up front. Sometimes a birth mother and father could come in and look through the adoption resumes of his clients. If the birth parents did not see a couple they were happy with, he would show them the "freebies." We were in that pile since we were making our own contacts as well.

In April 1989, we got a call from the attorney. He said that an East Indian birth mother had just come in. She had seen our adoption resume and wanted to meet us. She told us that she chose us because we seemed genuinely interested in having an integrated family, and we already were one. We drove up to Sacramento, and met with her. Ron laughed at me when we went out to lunch with her. I ordered curried chicken, and Ron said I did it to impress her. Very funny. For me, it was my dream come true. When I was in Guyana, I always loved to see the East Indian children and the black children, looking like flowers in their bright clothing. And I had dreamed of adopting, even as a child. We all got along, and started making our plans. She was due in July. Since I was also trying artificial insemination, for a few days, I thought I might also be pregnant but we wanted to go ahead with the adoption in any case. I found out I wasn't pregnant. On July 21, I went to Fresno with some of my friends to attend a pro-choice demonstration. Ron saw me on television at the protest and then he got the call. My son's birth mother went into labor and was on her way to the hospital. The moment I got home from Fresno, we hopped in the car and drove to Sacramento. We looked at all the beautiful babies in Sutter Hospital. My husband said, "Which one is Raul?" I just laughed. I had found him – the handsomest boy, with jet-black hair and Indian looks – no question about it. My husband was amazed that I found him so soon.

The birth mother had left instructions to be wakened when we got there. We spoke briefly, and hugged. We came back the next day. After she was dressed, she took a photo with our shared son. We talked about meeting up with her when he turns 18. Our son was long – 21 inches and so handsome. He had beautiful shiny black hair, and dark eyes so deep that you felt you could see his soul or your own soul in the reflection. Ron and I brought him home. We were ecstatic. We were also inexperienced and awkward. But with our Synanon friends, we learned how to wrap him in swaddling clothes, and walk him, and all the rest.

We also learned to ignore people at times. I would take Raul into our communal living room. At one end of the room, someone would tell me to wrap him up so he wouldn't get a chill. The next person would tell me I was suffocating him, and the next person would tell me to do something else. Advice all around. If I hadn't learned it before in my life, I certainly got a lesson about considering the source of any instruction or suggestion. In communes, everyone has an opinion.

Raul lived in Synanon during his first nine months, and was in daycare a few hours a day with the babies of our five other friends who had all adopted or birthed babies within the same three-month period. What a beautiful group of babies of all colors! We lived in a big mobile home on the side of a hill. You could look out the window and see deer, if you were very lucky. Or you could smell skunks from under the house, if you weren't so lucky. Raul swears he remembers the deer.

The Internal Revenue Service had been investigating Synanon to determine if it deserved its tax-exempt status. It finally judged that it did not qualify. After our unsuccessful appeals, the IRS began dividing up the assets and selling off property to pay off the millions of dollars of back taxes.

When Synanon disintegrated, opinions of former residents were all along the continuum from very positive and missing it intensely to very ready to be rid of it. My husband loved it there and would gladly have stayed. I was ready to move on. It depended on where you were in your life and what you were doing. Those who had to go out and live on social security were not funded properly. Those who were well trained with a good work ethic and young enough to start over were extremely successful. Most of the children who grew up on Synanon have done great things with their lives.

It was time for all of us to move out into the world. We had to learn a lot about basic lifestyle skills.

CHAPTER 12

All Alone in a Big World

We moved down from the hills and into Visalia about May 1990. We were living on our own for the first time in twenty years, while still having lots of great friends in close proximity. I had a night teaching job, and Ron was working days counseling at a nearby prison. Raul was with us most of the time and at a great daycare provider around the corner, for only a few hours a day. We rented a home for a year. Then in 1991, we bought our first home. After Raul was born, I decided I wanted to go into public school teaching so that I'd know what he should know, and I could help. Other than my Synanon friends, no one else in Visalia knew about my Peoples Temple experience. I kept it closed inside. In fact, once there were no more Synanon Games, I rarely spoke of Peoples Temple. I closed and locked that door. I would feel sadness in November, but rarely shared my pain.

One of the most enduring things I learned in Synanon was the "Act As If." Outside of a Synanon Game, we Synanon residents would simply do our jobs to the best of our abilities. We would "Act As If" we enjoyed it, liked everyone, felt fine and were content. We didn't whine or disrespect others. I may have been like that before, but I got the message that no one likes whining or complaining. I also know that it didn't accomplish anything. There is a time and place – in the Synanon Game – where you can do that. But in life, be positive, upbeat and focused. The "Act As If" got me through tough times. I had had a place to voice my pain, and I had had a place to try to keep it together. It worked for me. It was then ten years since I had returned from Guyana and moved into Synanon. The "Act AS If" strategy worked well for me.

Now I was moving out and I was more than ready to be on my own. I had learned a very important lesson. As long as I survived, I could keep going. I felt that I had moved mountains to survive the Peoples Temple ordeal, and nothing could ever be that hard for me again. As a group, though, we Synanon folks had a lot to learn. We had never bought cars, houses, insurance, groceries, or investments, nor had we ever put away money for retirement. We had to grow up quickly, do all our own chores and work hard on our jobs, too. We were very spoiled by Synanon. I even chuckled at times about parenting. I had worked with kids in both of the communities I had lived in, and never had a child in those often rich and exciting settings. Then, when I did have my child, there was no community. Ron and I were sole parents. Fortunately for us, Raul took it easy on us and has been such a bright treasure!

I quit my job teaching at the business college and started working for the Employment Development Department taking claims for unemployment. I went to school at night to finish off my bachelor's degree and, later, to earn my teaching credential.

One day, one of my co-workers at the Employment Development Office had a party for the office. I went and had a good time. I ended up spending most of the afternoon with my friend's 10-year-old daughter and the hostess' dog. My friend told me I should either be a veterinarian or a teacher – and we laughed.

At the employment office, a fellow employee there was a veterans' counselor. One day in the lunchroom, where we all had to eat if we brought our lunches, this counselor was furious about the "Don't ask, don't tell" policy of allowing gay soldiers in the military. He was angry and using slurs I couldn't live with. I took him aside and asked him to please control his temper and his language, and that he was offending me. I told him I had no choice but to share the staff dining room with him, and that he was out of line. He apologized. From then on, when anyone said something racist or biased (which still happened), people would immediately look at me to see if I had heard, if I had something to say, or if it was "safe." I have always hated living in a world like this.

Why can't people self-edit what they say – and ask themselves where their humanity is hiding?

I left as soon as I qualified to be a substitute teacher, on my long road to becoming a full-time teacher. I loved teaching and always seemed to move in that direction in any job setting. So while working, I finished the last thirty units for my Bachelors' degree (with dual majors of Philosophy/Psychology), and completed my Clear California Teaching Credential, with CLAD, a certificate for teaching language acquisition skills to students with non-English primary languages. I started teaching my first bilingual kindergarten class at the same time our son Raul enrolled in kindergarten. I taught in Tulare County for three years, and Raul had finished second grade.

As I moved from being an office worker into the field of education, one of my first jobs as a substitute teacher was in a class of middle school students who been kept from a great field trip because of consistently poor behavior. They ran me around in circles, hiding in cabinets, under sinks, in bookshelves – everywhere. I am surprised I didn't change my mind at that point. But no, I persisted. I got my first job as a bilingual kindergarten teacher on an emergency credential. At my first or second evaluation, the principal came in and sat down. All the kindergarten kids immediately went and sat on his lap. There went my "classroom management" plan. That was when I learned that the hardest part of teaching is classroom management. I have the smarts for the academic part, but behavior issues are the most challenging part.

At the end of my second year teaching bilingual kindergarten, my mother was diagnosed with lung cancer in July 1996, and died only a month later. I was able to stay with her that last month in Washington, D.C. and see her at the hospital every day. She had stayed with me through thick and thin, and helped me as much as she could when things were very hard for me. She was wonderful. I was so very delighted to be able to take care of her that last month. That was a gift for me. She was only 77 when she died.

When visiting my mother in the hospital, I asked a nurse for a lighter nightgown since my mom was so hot from her chemotherapy. The nurse said that she'd get to it as soon as she emptied the bedpan. I told her I had already done that. She was astounded. I think that my experience in Guyana – buying sides of beef and pork at the abattoir, cleaning smelly fish on the deck of a boat, planting and fertilizing crops – opened my eyes about having silly reservations about doing any kind of job. I could do it all. I didn't have to wait for a nurse to come and empty my own mother's bedpan.

My mom died in Washington, D.C., a city she loved and fought for over many years of her life. She had asked us to have her cremated, which we did. Linda, Ellen and I walked around Washington and put her ashes where she spent the most time, in front of the White House in Lafayette Park, protesting for home rule in the District, or to recognize Cuba and stop the trade sanctions, or for ending the war in Vietnam, at the Kennedy Center, around the Jefferson Memorial, by the parks where she walked, and around other political areas in the Nation's Capitol. We had a celebration of her life and gathered with her friends at her apartment complex. She had an eclectic group of friends; the only similarity was that they were all activists and passionate about at least one of her causes.

That same year, my father died of an aneurysm in Ft. Worth, Texas. We went down to his funeral, and our whole Texas branch of the family spent time together. They are a loving and inclusive group, especially my stepmother, who was also a great mother to both her own children and to my sisters and me. My father's ceremony was more traditional. He was not in the habit of going to church, but he ended up there, at his ceremony.

My son had taken his first step when I was visiting my mother in Washington, D.C. and I have a great picture of my father holding Raul when he was just a baby. It took me a while to get to a point that somewhat "normal" things were happening in my life. I am delighted that Raul met both of my parents. I only wished they hadn't smoked for nearly fifty years, so that they could have watched him grow up and he could know them. He was able to spend more time with Ron's parents, since they lived longer and we visited back and forth often.

At that time of my life, I had told no one about being in Peoples Temple other than my Synanon friends, the adoption agency and my son's birth mother. I couldn't take a chance that it would surface somehow and end things. I had to stay focused on what I was trying to accomplish. I still mourned on November 18. I still would be reminded by the news of "This day in history." I simply worked hard.

In Visalia, my family began our relationship with the Religious Society of Friends, commonly called "Quakers." During the first Iraq war over oil, Ron and I regularly demonstrated in downtown Visalia. We demonstrated against the war and generally met up with the same twenty folks from the Visalia area each week. We got along fine, and were delighted to find progressive activists in Visalia. Though many former Synanon residents lived in Visalia, there weren't many with us at these demonstrations.

A good friend of mine from Synanon, Judy Malcolm, adopted a beautiful two-year-old daughter as a single parent. Being a single parent is a huge job so we helped her all we could. She was and is a Quaker. She would pick up Raul and take him with her daughter to the Visalia Friends Meeting every Sunday. My husband and I would have a free morning. It worked out great for everyone. But then Judy remarried and moved away. So Raul would wake us up on Sunday, and say, "OK, I'm ready to go to Quaker Meeting." And, we took him. I have wanted him to be surrounded by progressives and pacifists and prefer those same people to be around me. Things have to be totally fair for Raul, and you have to do what you said you would do. Don't ask him to let you off the hook when you are sick or tired. He wanted no interruption in regularly visiting his friends at the Meeting and expected us to step up to the task of taking him. He developed a heartwarming relationship with an old Quaker named Ernest, and felt like he had a loving grandfather in Meeting. Since his routine was to attend the Quaker Meeting, he expected us to take him.

When we got to the Meeting the first time, there sat all of our fellow anti-war demonstrators, our Friends of the Library folks, and our Habitat for Humanity workers. We were immediately at home. We began attending there regularly. It was a beautiful experience. Unprogrammed Quakers have a quiet meeting, where you only speak if you are "led" to speak about a burning issue on your mind. The meeting is silent worship. No one leads a meeting or gives a sermon. Now, that was my kind of meeting. This was the absolute opposite from the Peoples Temple services. I feel like I internalized the frantic parts of Peoples Temple into my everyday life while I was there. More and more, I needed to calm the spinning of ideas in my brain. I wanted to appreciate my life because I had and have a very good life. I feel inundated by noise bombarding me from inside and out. I need to be quiet. I need to simply settle in my mind. On the other hand, there was no forum for me to mention I was in Peoples Temple. I felt like I was keeping a secret from my Visalia Quaker Friends, which felt uncomfortable to me. I didn't know how to remedy that.

Another uplifting part of that particular meeting was the location on the Quaker Oaks Farm, with peacocks, peahens, chickens, and old dogs walking by the full glass windows. My friends Bill and Beth Lovett lived on the farm and gave us a great place for Easter Egg Hunts and other fun activities. The kids had a perfect area for science experiments in their First Day School (children's program). On a lucky day, something would scare the peacocks, and they would open their exquisite tails like a fan. I have always appreciated the beauty of nature – like the Bird of Paradise plant along the path as I walked through Guyana's rain forest, and the full-spread tail of the peacock. I cherished those quiet, nurturing silences and I love those wonderful people who "speak my mind." That is a Quaker saying for someone who says the exact thing that I am thinking at the same moment. Another favorite saying with Quakers is, "I am a Quaker. In case of emergency, be quiet." Be calm and take care of business. I treasure that message. Many Quakers have a rich understanding of the Bible and work to understand it more. I totally agree with the "service" done by the Quakers, but will never have their curiosity about and love of the Bible. Regardless of the views I had about religion before November 18, 1978, any belief in a just God is gone forever.

We attended the Quaker Meeting in Visalia until we left in 1997. At this time, I was living a good life, and had accomplished my goals. I had some peace and some security that I had survived and had met the challenge of getting my life together. But the deep hole in my life was still there. Nothing had filled the gap I was living with.

CHAPTER 13
My Heart Was Filled Again

In 1997, big changes happened in our lives. My husband had worked for seven years through a private contractor as a counselor at a California prison. He liked it, but seemed sort of stuck. He started applying for jobs elsewhere and was hired as a Community Resources Manager at a prison in Calipatria, California. That position was directly under the warden, paid well, and had a lot of responsibility. Calipatria is off the beaten track in the southeast corner of Imperial County, two grueling hours east of San Diego in the desert. It was a limited-term job – a minimum of two years.

Besides that, my son had the very worst teacher I could imagine for second grade. I was disgusted with the Visalia School District for putting an unhappy sixth grade teacher in an over-crowded second grade class. She was a horror. Since I worked as a new non-tenured teacher in the same district, I felt my hands were tied. We were both ready for a change.

Ron was offered the job in Calipatria. We moved to neighboring El Centro, which had triple the population of Calipatria. I got one of the best jobs I've ever had at a local elementary school. I asked for Kindergarten, but the fabulous principal thought I'd be better suited for sixth grade, so I taught a transitional sixth grade class. I loved the staff and the students, and teaching sixth grade. We stayed there for the two years. As before, no one in El Centro knew anything about my past.

There were several highlights of living and working in El Centro.

One of my favorite fellow-teachers ran a limo business with her boyfriend. On my birthday, two years in a row, we gathered up folks and took a limo ride to the best local restaurant. It was totally delightful. The teachers at my school were truly terrific and the principal was effective and supportive. Another fabulous part was that my family traveled into Mexicali every Friday to eat at our favorite restaurant, "Los Arcos." We really appreciated the closeness to Mexico. The cultural exchange that was happening in the Imperial Valley area was great. And, our neighbors in the Calexico School System had brought some of the very best teachers to the area. It was a vital and exciting place to live nine months out of the year. The other three months, it was hot as hell. We enjoyed our two years in El Centro very much.

A drawback of moving to El Centro was that we had had to dislodge Raul from a very stable, familiar environment in Visalia. It was hard on him to leave his friends and relocate such a long distance away. I had certainly disliked his second-grade teacher and had thought so much about how relieved I was that I didn't notice how hard it was on him. His first year in El Centro was very tough. Eventually, Raul settled in some and blossomed in art classes and on a baseball team. He was making some nice friends by then. He takes his time making friends, but once he is sure of their loyalty, he is a friend for life. He greatly missed his friend, Sean, from Visalia. He made some good friends in El Centro but no one replaced Sean.

During this time, we tried to look up the Society of Friends (Quakers) once more. We found a Programmed Quaker meeting nearby which didn't meet our needs as well as the Visalia Friends Meeting, so we took a two-year hiatus. The Programmed Quaker Meeting was a Meeting led by a lay-minister. The Bible is read from and quoted, and psalms are sung. The members are not as geared to community service or to silence which I like. When I asked about what "community service" they were involved in, they didn't quite understand my question. I wasn't at home there.

While in El Centro, we got our first Internet access. I finally had the stability in my own life that allowed me to return to the puzzle of Jonestown. I began searching about Peoples Temple and bringing myself up-to-date about what was going on. I found Rebecca Moore's website and contacted her for the first time. She and her husband

Fielding McGehee had put a lot of work into the site called, "Alternative Considerations of Peoples Temple and Jonestown."

In early 1998 I re-opened my distant contacts with several Temple survivors, and found out that one of my closest Peoples Temple friends, Jim, was planning a 20-year anniversary party that year. Beginning with the very first year after November 18, 1978, a group had gathered at Evergreen Cemetery in Oakland. Evergreen Cemetery had courageously agreed to bury the bodies of hundreds of people who died in Jonestown in a mass grave. In 1979, cemeteries fought against giving the bodies a final resting place. It was a horror. Evergreen Cemetery stood out by its actions and all of the survivors and family members have appreciated their response to the crisis. Each year since then, though some different people attend, some stalwarts have come and organized the ceremony. I am so grateful that they did it. It took me twenty years to even get to their ceremony, but I have always appreciated that Reverend Jynona Norwood and her son have seen this through. Many of Reverend Norwood's relatives, including Fairy Norwood, died in Guyana. Reverend Norwood has worked tirelessly to get statewide and national recognition of those who perished. She presents a program each year, with music, speakers, a sermon, and other messages. Since she has been so diligent over all these years, I have enormous respect for her. However, as more of the survivors and their families come around looking for more answers, the need for a different kind of service has grown. We survivors didn't find solace in churches or in religion, for the most part. Those who did have a belief in a traditional religion before Jonestown felt abandoned by their churches. We gather in other more personal settings also but want to have a broader base for the service at Evergreen.

I had had very little contact with the other survivors over the past twenty years – sometimes going a year or more with none at all. I started thinking about attending the twentieth anniversary ceremony and the reunion afterwards.

I was fearful about making any contact because I didn't know what to expect. Shortly after I returned from Jonestown, one mother yelled and screamed at me and asked why I hadn't saved her son. I didn't know what the years had done to the memories of the other survivors or to relatives of those who died in Jonestown. I started going to a therapist in El Centro to work it all out. I wanted to go but I was scared to death. I had moved on in my life, but had the deep hole there. It was always nearby, but I didn't address it. I still had not told anyone outside of Synanon about my life in Peoples Temple. On each anniversary beginning in 1979, I would shut down and relive the tragedy alone. Even with those closest to me, it was too much to converse about. Early on, just anticipating that November was coming would make me very sad each fall. Later on, it was only during the month of November, then closer to the week of the eighteenth of November, and finally, on the eighteenth. Nevertheless, my whole calendar focused on November 18, from one year to the next. After weeks of therapy, I decided to go up to the ceremony and simply take a chance. I drove from El Centro to San Diego, flew up to San Francisco for the ceremony, and flew home the same day. I only wanted to put myself in harm's way for a twenty-four-hour period. I had too many fears about the experience to drag it out!

What an experience. As soon as I got there, I burst into tears. At the ceremony, I saw Stephan Jones, Jimmy Jones, and all the others. I hugged them and cried. Since then, I have watched many other survivors come for the first time – and Stephan and Jimmy always get the long hugs and tears. They are such treasures. Afterwards, we went to a nearby restaurant. I could not believe all the people there. Most had come to the reunion for the very first time as well. It was the twentieth anniversary, and we were all longing to reconnect with old friends. I saw people I had assumed were dead. After the tragedy and the continuing trauma, I couldn't remember exactly who died and who might have lived. I'd see a face in my dreams and not know with certainty about that person. Finally, I had just stopped trying to remember, at least during my waking hours.

Survivors had traveled many different paths. Some had been away from Jonestown for basketball, medical or other reasons, others had still been back in the states, and still others had left the Temple. Some of the survivors were children in the 1970s that had not gone to Guyana. Those of us who had miraculously survived and had been there were at the gathering too. Others had spouses or children go, and they were due to go soon, and still others had resisted going and either left the Temple or just had not made themselves available to go. Many were chomping at the bit to go, but their jobs had kept them in the States. There were lots of us. I had always thought of the survivors as being a handful. At the party, there were fifty or more. I was delighted, well hugged, and hugging everyone. It was a 100% positive day. That is not to say that we didn't grieve together. We did talk about those we missed so much, and about how much was lost. We talked about how we survivors had lived through the torture of it all. We communicated about our losses, our hopes, our survival, and ourselves. We talked a mile a minute about everything. The thing that was so moving about it was that we were out in the open; we were talking and reminiscing about a significant part of our lives that we had hidden for many years. Many old friendships were re-established. I got several of my best friends back after no contact for over 20 years and fearing for the worst. And, we kept the dialog going, and still do, to this day. Many of the survivors have had even more sorrows since the Jonestown deaths and have had to deal with that as well as the trauma of Jonestown. Tragedy has not left us alone. We needed to be together and to reconnect!

Some of the survivors who I saw that day had never been able to function back in the US society. They had reached the high point of their lives in Jonestown – being the most productive and responsible they had ever been before or since. Some had gone into recovery programs because they could thrive only in a closed community where you were held accountable and where you had a vision of where you wanted to go, and what your work could bring about.

Others had moved on. Before the gathering, my last mental pictures of the families and the survivors had been people at their darkest hours, painfully remembering their loved ones. Over the years, when I reflected on them, I still had those pictures. At the twentieth, I saw people who had big families, who smiled at times, who were gentle and kind, and who had bounced back to life. They hadn't forgotten – none of us could do that, but they had picked up their lives and rebuilt. I especially remember how delighted I was to see Grace Stoen Jones. She had been so strong for so long, a single voice raising life and death issues. She took Jim on, with all the resources he had. She had pursued getting physical custody of her son John, with no support from anywhere. She persisted with a stamina that was astounding. I was so happy that she had pulled strength from herself and she had a family again. More than anyone else, she gave me a wash of positive healthy thoughts. We reestablished our friendship from twenty-five years earlier, when we were neighbors in the Temple and both worked at the welfare department.

We all felt that finally we could talk about our tragedy and try to understand more about exactly how the tragedy happened. That was early on in my understanding of it all. I knew very little about the behind-the-scenes activity in Guyana, and have learned so much at each of the many gatherings since that time. I have definitely learned how much I was oblivious about, and what I should have seen had I merely opened my eyes. Wisdom and understanding have come to me at a snail's pace, though.

I felt my whole heart open up to swallow my old friends, and I felt other hearts open to me and to others. We didn't look for our differences even though there were many. There were those who judged Jim severely and those who gave him a pass. I felt then, and still do, that each of us had a unique experience in Peoples Temple. I can't judge choices or the opinions voiced by others. I can only, finally, be very glad that I survived. And, it also gave me the strength to assume the additional weight of clarifying some of the misconceptions of Peoples Temple.

One of the most poignant moments for me was speaking to other survivors about what their last twenty years had been like, since Jonestown. All of the stories of parents who had lost their children in Jonestown were so very tragic. None of us is without guilt. I knew that when I decided to make the choice to live through the pain, I had to admit that I was partially responsible for what happened. I should have seen it coming; I should have been more critical. One of the things that allowed me to eventually move on was thinking about those who died, those who were my soul mates. If I had died and another had survived, I would never have wanted the survivor to drown in the sorrow. I couldn't change what happened, no matter what I did now. All I could do was live a good life, work to make people treat people better, make the world more humane, and remember the dedication of my lost friends and our lost community.

When I went home to the counselor, I told her about the trip. I didn't need to go back to her – I had a big part of my family back. We survivors forgave each other for whatever had happened. We were all accomplices in our own ways. We all disregarded our inner voices that tried to warn us. I am sure of that. But life goes on. We either must decide to go on with ours, or not. No sitting on the fence. You're all in, or all out.

In 1999, the twenty-first anniversary, I somehow talked myself out of returning to Oakland. Since I'd gone on the twentieth and it had been great, I figured I'd jumped that hurdle. When that date arrived, when it was too late to make plans—I already knew that that had been a huge mistake. I couldn't believe I'd missed the anniversary in Oakland. I wrote to Grace Jones right away and explained that I had basically blown it. I told her I'd be there next year for sure. She wrote back that I was her first RSVP for the next year. I am happy, and lucky, to have her as my friend! I kept my promise to myself and that was the last anniversary I missed. I have never missed, nor do I plan to miss, the anniversary ceremonies at the Oakland Evergreen Cemetery.

My husband's two years at Calipatria were up. A new warden came in with his own staff. We only had to decide if the Imperial Valley, easily the hottest part of the California desert, was where we wanted to settle and buy a house. The three summer months in El Centro, July through September, were unbelievably hot. It was too hot to go shopping to more than one store at a time. Friends would visit us and opt for peanut butter sandwiches rather than go out in the heat, even to a tasty restaurant. Even union negotiations would be suspended over the summer because anyone who could leave town did so.

My husband and I are employable folks. We are bilingual, hardworking and passionate about our lives, so we figured we could live anywhere. Since he is an avid sailor, we opted to move to San Diego. I researched schools and made applications to different schools.

I spent a long time looking for a school for Raul. I wanted an elementary school with a sixth grade, not a middle school. I thought that would fit his personality better. I had some other qualities I was looking for, too. I found the right school in Fallbrook, a small community of about 32,000, close to San Diego. I applied and got a job teaching sixth grade in Fallbrook. Raul went to the same school for the two years I taught there. We commuted from Escondido together each day, which was another benefit of the job. The trip took about a half hour, and we both enjoyed our time talking, listening to his World War II audiotapes, arguing, or him reading. I thought of it as quality time away from chores, home, television, and telephones (before cell phones). At first

I taught sixth grade, then a combination fifth and sixth grade class of English immersion. Most of the students were learning English as their second language. I liked the school in many ways, and my son had his best teacher ever while in that school. That is certainly one of the perks of teaching at the same school as your child attends. I knew the best teachers and could put in my request for a particular teacher. Although it is not encouraged, or acknowledged, it is known to happen that a teacher's child is placed in a requested class.

Raul continued in the Fallbrook schools for another six years until he finished high school. He loved school, never argued about going, never got sick, and had extremely good friends. For the little inconvenience of getting him up there, twenty miles away, it was worth it.

After two years at this school, in 2000, I took a job as an administrator and teacher for a middle school literacy program through the California libraries. It was a fabulous job and a gratifying program for second-language learners. We took field trips around southern California and had enrichment activities and computer classes for the students. We also taught comprehension and reading skills.

In November 2000, I attended and spoke at the twenty-second Peoples Temple Anniversary Ceremony. It was the first time I had spoken. The ceremonies I have attended were religious, with Bible references and sermons. I am a practicing humanitarian, not a theorist, and not even a believer. I am at home with the Quakers. The Peoples Temple Anniversary ceremony framed in such religious terms did not speak to me or for me. Often I felt that the same hypocrisy that had brought Dr. Norwood's family and others away from their own churches and to Peoples Temple in the first place was very evident—too evident, to me.

At the ceremony, every person who spoke was totally negative about Jonestown and the lifestyle there. I knew that was not the case. I know the horrific way it ended is unchangeable and forever. Still there were many things we learned in Peoples Temple. For the most part, those of us in Guyana were visionaries who wanted a better life for our families, the world, and ourselves. Some gave up great fortunes, or the potential of great fortunes. All of us gave up our creature comforts for an unknown, new, and at first, inadequate community, because we wanted drastic changes in the world.

I stood at the podium on November 18, 2000, and said my truth (in tears, of course). I said that I would never have left Jonestown. I felt that was my home. I also said that most of those who died in Jonestown wanted to stay there, but that the tragic ending of Jonestown silenced their voices. If Jim had not decided to take everyone with him, if he had allowed others to take over leadership, if he had allowed those who wanted to leave to simply go, then, Jonestown could still exist, with those of us who loved it there. I have always felt that 85-90% of the people living in Jonestown loved it and would have been delighted to stay – especially without Jim's harangues. I told the audience that I felt that they should know that their loved ones were not miserable and enslaved. They were content in that beautiful part of the world. I felt I had to speak for them since they weren't here to speak for themselves. That is what I told the crowd.

Jonestown was an experimental society. We tried to brainstorm issues and conflicts, and be "everything to everyone" and we made mistakes along the way. We all merely wanted to fix the problems and keep on going. Those who were leaving with Ryan, who had left already, or who did not go to Guyana, definitely had their own perspectives. Their perspectives are the ones most available to the media. If you would ever assume that everyone in Peoples Temple was identical and mindless, simply listen to us now. We survivors vocalize every possible point of view. We are feisty, strong, passionate, and no-nonsense. Little things don't get to us; we have transcended the fluff in our environment.

At that ceremony, I met my beloved friend, Michael Bellefountaine. He was researching a book on the gay members of Peoples Temple entitled <u>A Lavender Look at Peoples Temple</u>. His observation took my breath away. He didn't know me at the time, but when I got up to speak, as he told me later, he thought, "Here I am sitting in this religious service, which seemed the anathema to most Temple members. And then, this white woman stood up and said that she loved Jonestown and never would have left. She offered a whole other picture of Guyana." The part that caught me off guard was that he called me "white." Somehow, when I was in the Temple, involved in Temple functions, I didn't think of myself as a color. I solely thought of myself as a Temple member. We had a different mind-set about skin color in the Temple, and it isn't the same in any other activity or gathering. I felt painted by the same paintbrush and the same color as others in the Temple. We were a unique group of people all of the same hew. I found out later that Michael had a terminal illness and that he relished contact with those of us who survived because he too wanted to focus on the essence of life and not the minutia that so many get bogged down in. He loved that we were openly discussing the depth of despair but kept on making the decision to have rich lives. He never spoke of his, but felt comfortable merely sitting with us. He instantly connected with many of us who had survived. Unfortunately, Michael died before he could finish his book but his efforts and his insight were so awesome. I still really miss him.

At several of the ceremonies since then, I have repeated statements along the theme that many loved their lives in Jonestown, as I did. I have also responded to numerous relatives of those who died in Jonestown. We have emailed each other, spoken on the phone or in person, or I have mentioned them in my interviews with different media representatives and researchers. This is the part of the story that is told less often because most of those who could tell it died in Jonestown.

Each year at the ceremony, or afterwards in someone's home, more of the survivors come out of the closet and identify themselves as former members. It isn't easy, and it isn't lightweight, but everyone I have spoken to feels that it has filled up an ache that we all carried alone until we gathered. We lost our families, our friends, and our vision of a better world, all on one day. Our friendships have been rekindled and they have significantly and positively affected our lives. It is a "sweet and sour" experience because you have to remember friends to enjoy the depth of the relationships, but then you reflect on so much more. Then it becomes painful. Some people have chosen not to engage in these gatherings and prefer meeting one-on-one, or in smaller groups. I am generally restless and sleepless before the gatherings, and sleep soundly afterwards. It helps me to know I am not forgetting my lost friends.

At every ceremony, new (old member) faces come. Many first-timers just observe us. But it is a first step. Many relatives – children of those who perished and children of the survivors – contact us through the website, "Alternative Considerations of Peoples Temple." They want to know how to help other family members, or how to help themselves. I know that all children need all the love they can receive, and so do we – those of us who have suffered this trauma. It simply feels better to communicate with someone who truly understands.

Some people come around reluctantly. They don't know what to expect from the rest of us. Some make their contact with us, but it is too late. One of my friends, Bobby Stroud, survived because he was injured in an accident in Jonestown and was sent to the hospital in Georgetown. When he came back to the United States, he tried to heal himself and never made any contact. He looked some of us up around the twenty-fifth anniversary. He died shortly after contacting us. Many of us felt we could have been some comfort to him if we'd had more time with him.

I had one experience that epitomized the ignorance surrounding Peoples Temple. I was visiting a counselor with my son. My son was proud of me so he talked to people about it. He even wrote a report in high school, with all the research done on the Internet. He mentioned it to the counselor, who made some comment. Then we moved on in our discussion. In a following visit, Raul mentioned we had been arguing about something on the way to the appointment. The doctor looked at us and told Raul, "Don't ever get in arguments like that with your mother. She might give you poison to drink!" After the session, I went home and called the "doctor." I read him the riot act and we changed doctors. The ignorance was astounding – and his flippant comment so offensive. Over the years, I tried not to cry myself into a river at every mention of Peoples Temple, but my cover was only skin-deep. It was often a struggle to keep up appearances. I always feel better after I address offensive ignorance.

I was rarely able to find the deep trust I had with my Temple friends. I developed many friends over the years, but only a handful knew the real me. I was guarded and selected very few to get behind my armor. People who have been abused or who have had difficult experiences in their lives keep things hidden in the same way. For all of us, finding a setting to be totally honest is our paradise.

In 2003, California entered into the budget crunch time. My program with California libraries was not funded, and no promises were made about the future of the program. I had started teaching English as a Second Language at night as a second job. I kept that, and did other miscellaneous consulting and teaching jobs, in business colleges, for the Job Corps, and in elementary schools. I started substituting and was picked up to do a long-term teaching assignment. My principal and I truly got along, and he hired me full-time for the next year (and the year after that, too). When he offered me the job, he said, "I have looked at your whole background, and I definitely want to offer you this job!" Since paranoia runs rampant in my brain, I wondered if he in fact looked into my background, or if he simply thought he did. I taught English immersion and remedial math classes to fourth and fifth graders. I love teaching upper elementary kids, and feel I am well placed, challenged, and excited by this job. I continue to teach upper elementary and middle school in this same school district.

CHAPTER 14
Friends, My Dear Friends

These ceremonies at Evergreen Cemetery in Oakland are very important to many of the survivors, friends, and family members. Former members who have been out of contact with the rest of us find out about the services and make their first contacts there. Afterwards, we can hug them and support them as they come to terms with being back with dear friends. There are many other benefits that emanate out of that ceremony. It stops us in our busy lives and gives us time and space to recollect and communicate about those loved ones we lost. I didn't have any blood-relatives die in Guyana. However, my handpicked adopted family members and the best friends I ever had, died. I mourn with others who lost their loved ones. We all miss them. On the eighteenth of every November, we send our love to them. Each year at the ceremony, more survivors, who keep a loose contact with one or another of us, come to pay their respects. Many came for the first time, twenty years after the deaths. Each year, more new faces show up and are embraced by the rest of us. The media come for the first ten minutes, take some photos and leave. They miss the whole thing. There is Reverend Norwood's ceremony in the background, as the survivors arrive and try to slide in, unseen. At times, one or more of us speaks.

As the ceremony becomes more religious, more pointed, and more doctrinaire, we survivors drift off towards the back. We hug, cry, converse, meet families, share stories and merely "be" there in that hallowed place. At the end, when we are ready, we leave to regroup in another, less public place – a restaurant, or a home. Since 2000, that has been the heart of our gatherings. We meet once a year around November 18, email from time-to-time during the year, and email furiously beforehand to make final plans. More recently, we have also begun to gather around the Fourth of July, in San Diego or San Francisco. People are able to pick which kind of gathering meets their needs. I go to all of them, because afterwards, I feel warmth of the connectedness of all my friends. Also, I simply can't take a chance that I would miss meeting up with someone who had never attended before. We were black, brown and white activists and idealists and had been zealots in the Temple, thirty years ago. We want to re-connect with our friends.

In 2001, changes began in the natural perception of Peoples Temple. In anticipation of the twenty-fifth anniversary, different scholars and researchers were pulling together programs to reflect on the movement. In August of 2001, David Dower of the Z Space Studio in San Francisco approached Leigh Fondakowski, who was the lead writer of *The Laramie Project*, and they worked out a plan for a Peoples Temple theater project. *The Laramie Project* told the tragic story of Matthew Shepard, a University of Wyoming student who was tortured and murdered near Laramie, Wyoming. He had been targeted because he was gay. The public outcry about the murder, helped along by Leigh's play, resulted in strong anti-hate crime legislation. Leigh brought a deep-rooted integrity and sensitivity to the project.

David called a group of folks together to discuss the project, including his wife Denice Stephenson, who was an ambassador of goodwill and a volunteer on the Peoples Temple collection of the California Historical Society's Peoples Temple Collection. He also included Tanya Hollis, another CHS staff member, Leigh Fondakowski, her co-writer Margo Hall, Paul Van de Carr who was working on a film, and Rebecca Moore and Fielding McGehee of the "Alternative Considerations of Jonestown" website. A group of survivors came too – Stephan Jones, Jimmy Jones, Kris and Bryan Kravitz, Grace Jones, Yulanda Crawford Williams, Leslie Wagner, Mike Cartmell, and me. The survivors included black and white, Jonestown and Georgetown residents, San Francisco residents, and those who fled from Jonestown. It was a diverse group, and our first conversation, face-to-face. In truth, the survivors expressed every possible point of view. Some had talked to the media earlier, and had been outraged by the distortions printed. Others had stayed quiet over the years. Some had loved Peoples Temple and were there at the end. Others had seen the cracks forming and had gotten out in time. The group represented how Leigh and David wanted to proceed – not hearing one voice, but many.

That was the first sign, in fact, that things were about to pick up. Leigh and Greg Pierotti, another of the writers, came out to interview me several times. Over the next two years, local newspapers and radio stations such as NPR, PBS, and Anderson Cooper from CNN interviewed me.

In the Bay Area, some local TV shows also got in touch with me. There was a renaissance of thinking about Jonestown. People weren't afraid to air that there had been many positive things. At this point, we had some experience to work with. The media had always taken the easy road to tell about Jonestown and Peoples Temple, rather than seeking out other perspectives. It was time to broaden their coverage. Many of the documents that could clear up questions about Jonestown were still held by the FBI, which was reluctant to release them. Nonetheless, it had released some tapes and documents, which verified other memories, and created more conversation. There was government involvement in Jonestown and in Peoples Temple, to an unknown extent, but the government was most certainly monitoring the activities.

It was time to look at the story in more depth. More and more people were researching the enigma of Peoples Temple, and to a much deeper extent. Many more of the survivors and the families of those who died were willing to talk more freely about what had drawn them there, what it had been like, and how they reflected upon it now. Friendships that had lain dormant over the years became important and made meaningful conversations happen all around. The *Jonestown Report*, new books, new research, and current interviews were raising the interest levels of the public. People had survived the shock of November 18 and the trauma of living through it, and had moved on rebuilding their lives, but still felt the ache of friends lost. Each survivor and relative had a story, a personal story, of his or her time in or relationship with Peoples Temple. Each of us had survived, reflected, remembered, and synthesized the experience into our lives, and the result was a panorama of thoughts and feelings.

The twenty-fifth anniversary, with the Z Space Studio push, the play, another historical film in the works, the California Historical Society, the survivors who came out of the closet, the further research, the communication between survivors, other media attention – all of that opened a whole new conversation. There was discussion about the real happenings in Peoples Temple, both good and bad. We all found out bizarre and unbelievable things that had been secret and hidden. We all found out things about each other that drew us together even more. It was okay to have been in Peoples Temple. It literally went from something you'd be reluctant to bring up with good new friends, to something you'd share, even though you had to listen to the predictable misinformation that most people had and have. It was still okay. There was a new permission granted to clear the air – and many people told their families and friends about being part of Peoples Temple. It was time to open up and share our hidden thoughts.

Books have been written, and Leigh's play was performed at the Berkeley Rep, in Alaska, at the Guthrie Theater in Minneapolis, and at the Perseverance Theater in Chicago. Denice Stephenson edited a moving book, *Dear People*, with documents and memorabilia from the Peoples Temple archives at the CHS. The *Jonestown Report* continues to grow as scholars, researchers, survivors, family members, and critics write for the annual periodical. Stanley Nelson and Noland Walker put together an acclaimed documentary, *The Life and Death of Peoples Temple* that has played at many venues around the country to sold-out theaters, winning numerous awards. And, more books, more articles, more interviews keep coming.

In my own life, since coming to San Diego, I've been able to connect a lot with Rebecca Moore, Fielding McGehee, and John Moore. They are my adopted family – they lost their family members, Annie Moore, Carolyn Layton, and Carolyn's three-year-old son.

My family has found Quakers again and we lovingly protest the daily atrocities that we see committed against fellow world citizens, and share a better vision for the future. I am still teaching and loving it. My husband of twenty-nine years is selling computers.

My son has been amazing to watch. Over the years, he has attended many Peoples Temple events with me, has met many of my best friends, and has watched the process of our coming together. Now he has stepped into the middle of things. He went with me to watch one interview I had with the BBC, in Hollywood. He wrote a high school research paper on Peoples Temple. When he decided to research Peoples Temple, he wanted to use all of his own sources. I offered to contact Jimmy and Stephan, but he declined my help. He wanted to do it in his own way, to understand things he was researching, and to come up with his own slant on my story. He went with me to the opening of Stanley and Noland's movie, at the San Francisco International Film Festival. He looked me up on the Internet, and showed my picture to several of his teachers, and included it in a report. He has mentioned my story to others in his life (for better or for worse). At his university, we jointly hosted a presentation about Jonestown and Peoples Temple. He is proud of me, and curious about where I've been. He is a World War II historian, but is interested in human rights and news of the world. He has an inquiring mind, and always wants to get past the easy explanations of things and delve into their real meaning.

Nothing has replaced Peoples Temple for me. During my time in Peoples Temple, it was the purest, most service-oriented time of my life. It was a twenty-four-hour-a-day calling and there was no downtime for me. I was enchanted by my impact on my world and the larger community around me. I was never bored, idle, sucked into trivia, superior, or unfulfilled. My life was overflowing because I could see the result of my daily efforts on the community around me. Peoples Temple was a residential haven for the downtrodden and for the idealists who were tired of working alone. It picked us up, carried us along, and worked our tails off to persuade us not to give up.

Since I came back in 1978, there have been several times that my reaction to things happening around the world was significantly influenced by my time in Peoples Temple. For example, in the early 1990s, the Branch Davidians and David Koresh were slaughtered in their home near Waco, Texas. When I heard the news about the slaughter, I was crushed. Their ideology did not touch me, nor did most aspects of their lives. But I did see them as "family" in that they had followed a path that was more real than the plastic malls, the pre-fab everything around us, and the superficial level of the lives that many people live. They lived together, the most reasonable way to live from my point of view, and cared about each other. They had developed their own extended adopted family. Living communally is not easy. Ex-Synanon friends of mine in co-housing find that many issues need to be settled there, even in the more detached, private settings. Yet the Branch Davidians, as the Temple members, felt the effort was worth it. Of course, the other similarity was that so many died needlessly.

A second time that my Peoples Temple experience gave me a different perspective was during and after Hurricane Katrina. As the hurricane and floods were sweeping the southeastern United States, and especially Louisiana, we were all able to watch it unfold on the television. The inhumanity with which we treated the victims was appalling and unforgivable. It was so awful because no one ran to remedy the situation! I simply couldn't believe that people were so inept and so unfazed, and had no resources in place that they could call on. During that time, I thought a lot about how Jim had gathered effective and efficient people around him. We were all hard workers, and we would not leave a job unfinished. No one should ever have abandoned those people. My point is that people too easily judge that something is impossible to remedy. It would have been intolerable for him to watch, and he would have fixed it. He would have come up with a plan, moved mountains and embarrassed presidents to get those conditions reversed. He would have mobilized private planes, movie stars, or politicians. He had a general survival instinct that went beyond himself to those he loved and cared for, all people of color and people in need. I have no doubt that he would have changed things so that disgrace wasn't allowed to happen in the first place, much less to continue. My comments are not to reflect positively on Jim Jones, but to reflect negatively on those with power who could ignore the unfolding tragedy. Our society has to stop allowing it. There is a way to rectify any situation. Just do it. Move that mountain, and resolve the crisis. It absolutely could have been fixed in a timely and effective way. I did learn that no challenge was insurmountable. If one person could successfully move a thousand people to the remote, undeveloped center of South America, another with the resources available to the a congressman or senator, or especially, president of the United States could certainly figure out how not to abandon citizens of our country. They gave up too easily.

A friend recently asked me to speak to his daughter who had joined a cult. I have such mixed feelings about the whole issue of deprogramming. I almost think that deprogramming a person from a cult is somewhat like getting an addict to stop using drugs or alcohol. Nothing can be done until that person makes the choice. No helpful friend or family member can do it. A person must have some recognition that they are losing something they want or need in order to allow deprogramming. When I lived in the Temple, how would deprogramming have affected me? I would have resisted it because I was driven to find out whom I was, and I had to make lots of mistakes to get there. I had a bit more life experience than some other young white women in the Temple at that time, but was missing the insight from my experiences. Once settled into the Temple life, I really flowered. I don't think that deprogramming would have worked for me. The other issue has to do with the reason someone would want you deprogrammed. What is that person's motivation? I might find reason to distrust a person who either "programmed" or "deprogrammed" another. When I have seen deprogrammers interviewed, I have not been impressed with their integrity. I would want to understand the motivation behind both.

Another issue when talking or thinking about "cults" is that the word is used so broadly that it ceases to be meaningful. If a cult is a group that controls the group consciousness and requires complete dedication, there are many such groups around. You could include the Marines, boy scouts, and some religions, which even advise which candidates to vote for, or not to vote. Our society is full of groups that work to sway the behavior and opinions of the members. Peer pressure is used in all kinds of settings. In Synanon, the Synanon Game was used to effect change in behavior at times. Was it bad? I saw miracles happen when offenders and addicts came to important realizations about their actions.

I recently caught myself thinking that Peoples Temple members were unique. I am finding that as we meet more and more people we collect "wannabe" Peoples Temple folks. As journalists, friends, colleagues, media folk, ex-spouses, parents and family members who lost loved ones, meet us, they like us and understand us. I can't tell you how many college students work tirelessly transcribing tapes, or journals, or radio logs. Many middle school and high school students contact us to do reports on Jonestown and the Temple. These students are doing such in-depth studies that they are winning national awards. Afterwards, they keep in touch. The shallow interpretations of what happened in Jonestown and the Temple don't ring true, and authors who have already proven that they want to delve into the deepest secrets have come around to do articles and books. It is gratifying!

Lately, I've realized that the world is made up of many special people. Some may never hear of Peoples Temple, but they are still the "type" of person that a Peoples Temple person would love, or enjoy spending time with. Some are teachers, some are Quakers, some are farm workers, and some are veterans – a big mix. Those are the people who make life so special.

In her book *Orange Crushed*, by Pamela Thomas wrote:

At different points in my life, I have been convinced that there are only two kinds of people in the world. At one point, I thought it was blacks and whites, then I thought it was men and women; later I became convinced that it was Democrats and Republicans. But now I know that there are really are only two kinds of people in the world, those who have experienced a permanent personal loss, and those who haven't.

I absolutely agree with that. I also know that there are many tragedies in the world, and that we are all touched by them. No one has a life without sadness. However, for me, the words "permanent personal loss" mean that you question whether the next step is worth it or not. The pain is simply too much. And then, you are forced to move on.

I passed through that period, and it took years, not days or weeks or months. And now, with that as my foundation, I have chosen life. Most days, I am above the fray of daily life. I have simplified things I worry about. I make it a point to help make the world a better place. I try not to be compromised by our society and world. I can't tolerate racism, sexism, or deception by elected officials or anyone else. I also can't tolerate violence, war, or bullying, whether it is personal or institutional. It has made me who I am today, and it will take me where I'm going tomorrow. My friends and my desire for a better world make my life full and rewarding. I'm so glad that I made that choice about thirty years ago, to keep on keeping on.

My friend Sonja has been my good friend since I met her in Synanon and edited this book. She made me laugh. I wrote a sentence about wanting to exercise my "courage" muscle and that I never wanted to be passive again. She asked me when was I ever passive. She couldn't remember a time. One of Jim's secretaries once wrote a note to Jim about me, while I was living in Georgetown. She said that I was the most passive person she had ever met. Back then, I was so overwhelmed with the richness of my life in the Temple that I had no need to be anything but passive. I know now that I was not seeing a lot of what was going on with Jim, or with others who were unhappy in the Temple. I do think that I was too passive, as well as naïve, unobservant, idealistic, and optimistic. I so wanted to have a world where people were treated with dignity.

In many ways I am the same person I always was. Some kind people say I look the same. Some might even think I am totally the same. But I'm not. I can move mountains, I can accomplish a lot. I can keep on living and have a good life. I can laugh, have fun, cry, and know myself. But I can never completely forgive myself. I can never forget what we had and what Jim's insanity and illness swept away. I can never forget how strong I am to have survived and to have a meaningful life and treasured family.

I am not the same inside. I wouldn't want to be the same. I wouldn't want to have learned nothing. But I like who I am today. I love that my life has been so peculiar and so significant. When I look to the future, I think about what my niche is. I know that there are very few survivors, and even fewer who talk freely about the pain we have shared. But I feel better when I address it. I want to clarify misconceptions and give a face and a voice to my friends who have died. My future looks as busy as my last thirty-one years have been.

Tombstone for many of the wonderful people who died in
Jonestown. Evergreen Cemetery, Oakland, California.

California Historical Society Peoples Temple Exhibit, where survivors gather
each year to identify photos and spend time with memories of our loved ones
who perished. The CHS is at 678 Mission Avenue, San Francisco, CA 94105.

CHAPTER 15

And What is on the Horizon?

Where do I go from here? My life is very full now, with my husband of twenty-nine years, my college-aged clever son, my class, my Quaker work, my Peoples Temple connectedness, and my activism. I think I do want to return to Jonestown one final time. I am still in love with it. I know that it can't be the same ever again. Visiting any place as a tourist is so very different from living there and doing all the day-to-day things. But, I still want to go.

In addition, the California Historical Society still has many documents and unidentified photos, which I would like to go through and try to identify. I get nourishment by identifying these faces. I loved them a lot. There is still information to get out about the people of Jonestown. So much is known – or thought to be known – about Jim. He has monopolized the media and air space so that other jewels have not been appreciated. I'd like to continue doing that by my interviews and my work with Peoples Temple survivors. We gather in November, focusing on the ceremony at Evergreen Cemetery, and we gather in a smaller, more intimate group, each July.

I've never yet been able to guess what might come next anywhere along the line. In November 2008, Fox News interviewed me for a show on survivors. A good friend was recently interviewed on the Montel show. Oprah interviewed Jimmy Jones in February 2010. I am in communication with several college, high school, and middle school students on their research projects, Relatives and friends of members contact me frequently, along with individuals who want to get a better understanding than the superficial coverage presented by the mainstream media. I have started to make annual presentations at the Communal Studies Association Conferences. Here, scholars who have studied historical communities around the world and especially in the United States, gather to discuss and broaden our understanding of those groups. I speak as a survivor of a contemporary community and have found a great deal of understanding within this group. In turn, they have taught me a lot of the communal dynamics. One of my presentations was published in the "Communal Studies Journal."

I am also working with Rebecca Moore and Fielding McGehee to upload identified photos from many sources onto the "Alternative Considerations" website and I am delighted to make these photos available to relatives and scholars.

And, finally, I have finished this book. I feel a responsibility that I have a unique perspective about the lives of those who died in Peoples Temple. I remember most of the names and faces and I want to share that information with their surviving family members. I want to get photos of people in Jonestown up on the website so everyone can see them and know them.

I continue to learn more hidden details about Peoples Temple and Jonestown. I recently found out that Jim had ordered the cyanide well before November 18, 1978. That means that there was no spontaneity in the deaths during Congressman Ryan's visit – it was all staged. I want to know who helped, since I know Jim was drugged and mentally ill. I want to know how we all got to that point that our involvement with a crazy man made us crazy too. I want to know why Jim wasn't stopped by people close to him and who saw what was happening. It doesn't change my dream of what Peoples Temple could have become. It does change how much I blame Jim and those who enabled him to take everyone with him. It was not a final act of a single crazy person. I have often quoted, "Power corrupts and absolute power corrupts absolutely," and I use it in reference to Jim. But, it wasn't only Jim. It was those around him who grew bold with importance. And, I am afraid that I am no different than any of them – not smarter, not dumber, and not more or less perfect. I saw notes that we all wrote over our years in Peoples Temple. In some ways the best was brought out of us, in some ways the very worst. What could I have done? It is very scary to me. I truly want to be self-righteous and say I would or could never... But I knew the people surrounding Jim so well. They started out with good intentions, as I believe he did many years beforehand.

I don't know exactly where we are heading. All I know is that it doesn't end here, not yet. I am more like you than you expected. Even I wouldn't do many of the things I did as a young person. I certainly tested my boundaries. I was very lucky and I survived. That simply means that I've learned through my years, as you have. I never learned my lessons vicariously. No one could advise me to refrain from one thing or another. I had to be in the mire myself. Now I am carving my way into the future. I take my own path. I stay true to myself. And I continue to grieve as I push ahead.

Laura and her mother, Virginia Reid

Lydia Kohl and Virginia Reid, Laura's mother-in-law and mother.

Raul, Laura, and Ron Kohl

Who Survived the Jonestown Tragedy?

Alternative Considerations of Jonestown and Peoples Temple
http://jonestown.sdsu.edu

The following is a list of Peoples Temple members who were in Guyana on 18 November 1978 and who survived the deaths in Jonestown, Georgetown, and the Port Kaituma airstrip. There are 87 individuals on this list. Those who are known to have died or who are presumed to be dead. Other names by which the survivors were known appear in lower case. Nicknames often the names by which they were known in Jonestown appear in parentheses after the given names.

Most of the people on this list were on survivors' lists printed in newspapers and/or prepared by the FBI and State Department in the weeks following the mass deaths. Other names appeared on lists prepared at the time by Laura Johnston Kohl and Jim Randolph. Since then, numerous people in addition to Jim and Laura have provided us with more information. We are especially grateful for the assistance of Don Beck, Tim Carter, and Denice Stephenson.

If you know of any changes that need to be made, either of additional survivors or of people known to have died, please contact us by email at fieldingmcgehee@yahoo.com, or by mail to Fielding McGehee, 3553 Eugene Place, San Diego, CA 92116.

Fielding M. McGehee III prepared this list, and updating is an ongoing project as new information is brought to Fielding. If you use this source, please credit the following: Alternative Considerations of Jonestown and Peoples Temple, http://jonestown.sdsu.edu. Thank you.

ADAMS, Paula 29

BAGBY, Monica 18
BARNETT, Carl Henry 22
BEIKMAN, Charles Edward (Chuck) 43
BEIKMAN, Thomas Charles (aka Thomas (Tom) Cutlass) 21
BLAKEY, George Philip (Phil) 25
BOGUE, Edith Elizayabeth 39
Bogue, Harold, see CORDELL, Harold
BOGUE, James Ernest (Jim) (aka Jim Morrel, Jim Murrel) 46
BOGUE, Juanita 21
BOGUE, Teena May (aka Teena Turner, Tina Turner) 22
BOGUE, Thomas James (Tommy) 17
BROOKS, Madeleine 73
BROWN, Stephanie (aka Stefanie Morgan) 10

CAMPBELL, Marion Anthony 61
CANNON, Henry, Jr. 18
CARTER, Michael Julien 20
CARTER, Timothy *James* 30
Casanova, Dianne, see SCHEID, Dianne
CASANOVA, Mary Ann Scheid 37
CLARK, Richard 41
Clarke, Diane, see LOUIE, Diane
CLAYTON, Stanley Roy 25
COBB, John Raphael (aka John Cobb Jones) 18
Connesero, Versie, see PERKINS, Versie
CORDELL, Harold (aka Harold Bogue) 41
CORDELL, Mark Nathan 19

DAVIS, Grover Cleveland 79

DE PINA, Miguel 84
DOUGLAS, Calvin 19

EVANS, Julius Lee 30
EVANS, Sandra 30
EVANS, Sharla 7
EVANS, Shirelle 5
EVANS, Sonya 11

FRANKLIN, Johnny, Sr. 33

GARDFREY, Dawn Francine (aka Dawn Mitchell) 15
GIEG, Clifford 18
GODSCHALK, Raymond O., Jr. 62
GOSNEY, Vernon Dean 25
Grubbs, Bea, see ORSOT, Bea

HENDRICKS, Aaron 25

INGRAM, Lee (aka Marion Lee Ingram, Mickey Ingram) 33
Ingram, Marion Lee, see INGRAM, Lee
Ingram, Mickey, see INGRAM, Lee

JANARO, Claire Elaine 39
JANARO, Richard Mario 51
JOHNSON, Ruby Neal (aka Ruby N. Williams Johnson) 56
Johnson, Ruby N. Williams, see JOHNSON, Ruby Neal
JOHNSTON, Laura Reid 31
Jones, *James Warren, Jr., see JONES, Jimmy, Jr.*
JONES, Jimmy, Jr. (aka James Warren Jones Jr.) 18
Jones, John Cobb, see COBB, John Raphael

JONES, Stephan Gandhi 19

Jones, Tim ìDayî, see TUPPER, Timothy Glenn

Jones, Timothy Tupper, see TUPPER, Timothy Glenn

KIRKENDALL, Chuck 30

Kutulas, Thomas (Tom), see BEIKMAN, Thomas Charles

LAYTON, Laurence (Larry) 32

LOUIE, Diane (aka Diane Clarke, Diane Louie Lund, Diane Louie Rozynko) 26

Lund, Diane, see LOUIE, Diane

MARTIN, Andrea Yvette (aka Andrea Yvette Walker) 21

McCANN, Paul 27

Mitchell, Dawn, see Dawn GARDFREY

MITCHELL, Guy Edgar 25

MITCHELL, Linda (aka Yolanda Denice Mitchell) 18

Mitchell, Yolanda Denice, see Linda MITCHELL

Morgan, Stefanie, see BROWN, Stephanie

Morrel, Jim, see BOGUE, James Ernest

Morton, Beatrice Alethia, see ORSOT, Bea

Murrel, Jim, see BOGUE, James Ernest

NEWELL, Cleveland, Jr. 23

NEWELL, Herbert 20

OíNEAL, Christopher Keith 21

ORSOT, Bea (aka Bea Grubbs, Beatrice Alethia Morton) 52

PARKS, Brenda 18

PARKS, Dale 27

PARKS, Edith 64

PARKS, Gerald 45

PARKS, Joyce 32

PARKS, Tracy 12

PAUL, Robert 33

PERKINS, Versie Lee (aka Versie Connesero) 32

PROKES, Mike 31 (Shot himself in March 1979)

PURSLEY, Joan 21

RHODES, Odell 36

RODRIQUEZ, Aurora 53

Rozynko, Diane Louie, see LOUIE, Diane

SATTERWHITE, Alvaray 61

SCHEID, Dianne Elizabeth (aka Dianne Casanova) 15

SIMON, Michael Angelo 23

SMITH, Eugene Erskin 21

Stahl, Robin see TSCHETTER, Robin Faye

STROUD, Robert Homer (Bobby) 21

SWINNEY, Helen Beatrice 65

THRASH, Hyacinth 76

TOUCHETTE, Charles E. (Charlie) 48

TOUCHETTE, Deborah Ruth (Debbie) 23

TOUCHETTE, Michael Jon (Mike) 25

TOWNES, LeFlora 56

TSCHETTER, Robin Faye (aka Robin Stahl) 21

TUPPER, Timothy Glenn (aka Timothy Tupper Jones, Tim ìDayî Jones) 19

Turner, Teena, see Teena May BOGUE

Turner, Tina, see Teena May BOGUE

WADE, Preston 23

WAGNER, Leslie (aka Leslie Monique Fortier Wilson) 21

Walker, Andrea Yvette, see MARTIN, Andrea Yvette

WILLIAMS, Walter L. 21

WILSON, Burrell Dernardo 18

WILSON, Jakari 2

Wilson, Leslie Monique Fortier, see Wagner, Leslie

YATES, Johnnie Mae (aka Nedra Yates) 54

Yates, Nedra see YATES, Johnnie Mae

Young, Carol Ann see YOUNG, Carolyn

YOUNG, Carolyn (aka Carol Ann Young) 78

Who Died in Guyana on November 18, 1978?

"Alternative Considerations of Jonestown and Peoples Temple," http://Jonestown.sdsu.edu.

Completed almost 30 years after the deaths in Guyana, the following is the first list to include the names of everyone who died in Guyana on 18 November 1978.

There were 918 people who died that day. Five (Rep. Leo Ryan, NBC correspondent Don Harris, NBC soundman Bob Brown, newspaper photographer Greg Robinson, and Temple defector Patty Parks) were shot to death at the Port Kaituma airstrip. Four (Sharon Amos and her children Liane Harris, Christa Amos and Martin Amos) died at the Peoples Temple house in Lamaha Gardens in Georgetown. The remaining 909 died in Jonestown.

Fielding M. McGehee III compiled this list from a number of different sources. These sources include: the U.S. Department of State list released on 17 December 1978; the U.S. House Foreign Affairs Committee report on the assassination of Rep. Leo J. Ryan, published 15 May 1979; the Jonestown/Guyana Memorial Wall Committee list prepared in October 1995; Peoples Temple records and censuses which the organization maintained in Jonestown; documents released under the Freedom of Information Act from the FBI in 2002; and individuals whose friends and relatives died on 18 November 1978.

Because the names on this list came from numerous and varied sources of information, there may still be some misspellings, duplications and other inaccuracies. In addition, where available, we have included each person's date and place of birth, and the last city, state, and zip code of residence; some of these may be incorrect as well. Finally, while we have listed relationships between family members in the biographical boxes for each person, we know we have missed some of the family connections. We would like to correct as many of these errors and oversights as possible. Please <u>CONTACT US</u> at http://Jonestown.sdsu. edu. with any corrections and additions that you believe we should include.

This list was updated 1 August 2008 and continues to change as I receive more information. If you cite this source, please give the following credit: "Alternative Considerations of Jonestown and Peoples Temple," http://jonestown.sdsu.edu.

A

ADDISON, Stephen Michael 5/4/1944 Santa Rosa, CA 95401

ALBUDY, Ida Marie 8/26/1906 San Francisco, CA 94115

ALEXANDER, Lillian Boyd 2/17/1906

AMOS, Christa 3/7/1967 Redwood Valley, California 95476

Amos, Krista, see AMOS, Christa

Amos, Liane, see Liane HARRIS

Amos, Linda, see Sharon AMOS

AMOS, Martin Laurence 4/19/1968 Redwood Valley, California 95476

AMOS, Sharon 7/4/1936 Redwood Valley, California 95476

Amos, Wayborn Christa, see AMOS, Christa

ANDERSON, Jerome Dwayne 10/30/1960 San Francisco, California 94115

ANDERSON, Marcus Anthony 7/29/1963 San Francisco, California 94115

ANDERSON, Marice St. Martin 7/22/1962 San Francisco, California 94115

ANDERSON, Orelia 6/8/1910 Los Angeles, California 90006

Anderson, Richardell Smith, see PERKINS, Richardell Evelyn

ANDERSON, Samuel Moses 4/12/1911 Oakland, California 94604

ANDERSON, Shantrell Akpon 11/7/1971 San Francisco, California

ANDERSON, Tommy Lee 12/25/1959 San Francisco, California 94115

ARMSTRONG, Oreen 10/11/1904 San Francisco, California

ARNOLD, Birdie 2/27/1907 Los Angeles, California 90003

Arnold, Luberta, see ARNOLD, Birdie

ARTERBERRY, Clarence 12/23/1973 San Francisco, California

ARTERBERRY, Linda Theresa 12/6/1948 San Francisco, California 94115

ARTERBERRY, Ricardo David 1/15/1968

ARTERBERRY, Traytease Lanette 4/6/1971 San Francisco, California

ATKINS, Lydia 10/4/1948 San Diego, California 92113

ATKINS, Ruth 3/4/1904 San Francisco, California 94113

Augustine, Dante, see Dante CARROLL

B

Backmon, Elaine, see Viola Elaine BACKMON

BACKMON, Viola Elaine 3/23/1950 San Francisco, California

BACON, Monique 4/6/1976 San Francisco, California

BAILEY, Geraldine Harriett 3/23/1912 San Francisco, California 94121

BAILEY, Mary Jane 9/6/1915 Los Angeles, California 90006

BAISY, James Samuel, Jr. 1/15/1965 San Francisco, California

Baisy, Jerry, see Jerry WILSON

BAISY, JonDeshi 9/27/1971 San Francisco, Claifornia

BAISY, Kecia 6/10/1966 San Francisco, California

BAISY, Shirley Mae 1/14/1945 San Francisco, California 94109

BAISY, Siburi Jamal 6/28/1969 San Francisco, California

Baisy, Trinidette, see Trinidette CORNNER

BAISY, Wanda 9/16/1963

BAKER, Eric Tyrone 4/13/1963 Los Angeles, California

BAKER, Jair Alexander 5/23/1959 Los Angeles, California

BAKER, Shawn Valgren 4/21/1965 Los Angeles, California

BAKER, Tarik Earl 10/29/1961 Pomona, California 91766

BALDWIN, Mary Be 4/8/1926 Los Angeles, California

BARGEMAN, Rory LaVate 6/21/1961 San Francisco, California

Bargeman, Terence Vair, see Terri BARGEMAN

BARGEMAN, Terri 11/3/1962 San Francisco, California

BARRETT, Becky Ann 3/8/1974 Ukiah, California 95482

BARRETT, Ben Franklyn 11/18/1934 Ukiah, California 95842

Barrett, Cathy Ann, see Cathy Ann STAHL

BARRON, Jack Darlington 11/9/1921 Redwood Valley, California 95476

BATES, Christine Ella Mae 3/22/1905 Ukiah, California 95482

BEAL, Geneva Mattie 9/4/1920 San Francisco, California

BEAM, Eleanor Marie 3/5/1961 San Francisco, California 94115

BEAM, Jack Lovell 11/25/1923 Ukiah, California 95482

Beam, Joe, see Joseph Leo HELLE III

BEAM, Rheaviana Wilson 8/15/1924 San Francisco, California 94117

BECK, Daniel James 5/15/1966 Redwood Valley, California

BEIKMAN, Rebecca May 11/29/1940 Redwood Valley, California 95470

BEIKMAN, Ronald La Mont 7/7/1966

BELL, Alfred 3/12/1909 San Francisco, California

BELL, Beatrice Claudine 2/3/1955 San Francisco, California

BELL, Carlos Lee, Jr. 11/8/1964 San Francisco, California

BELL, Elsie Ingraham 6/11/1918 San Francisco, California

BELLE, Ethel Mathilda 4/7/1890

Bender, Betty Jean, see Betty Jean FITCH

BENTON, Lena Mae Camp 11/24/09 Los Angeles, California

Benton, Lena Mary Camp, see Lena Mae Camp BENTON

Berkley, Yolanda Patrice, see Yolanda SOUDER

BERRY, Dana Danielle 6/8/1970 San Francisco, California

Berry, Daniel Bernard , see Danny McCANN

BERRYMAN, Ronnie Dewayne 2/26/1952 Los Angeles, California 90006

BIRKLEY, Julia 7/25/1909 Los Angeles, California 90611

Bishop, Jim Arthur , see Jimbo JONES

Bishop, Stephanie Lynn, see Stephanie JONES

Black, Mary Emma Love Lewis, see Mary LOVE

BLACKWELL, Odell 1/13/1910 Los Angeles, California 90003

BLAIR, Ernestine Hines 8/9/1917 Los Angeles, California 90037

Blair, Norya, see Norya QUINN

Blair, Ruthie , see Ruthie Mae QUINN

Bloom, Phyllis, see Phyllis CHAIKIN

BOGUE, Marilee Faith 3/31/1959

BORDENAVE, Selika Glordine 7/10/1918 San Francisco, California

BOUQUET, Claudia Jo 5/1/1956

BOUQUET, Pierre Brian 7/20/1953 Burlingame, California

Boutte, Corlis, see Corlis Denise CONLEY

BOUTTE, Mark Anthony 4/14/1957 San Francisco, California

BOWER, Donald Robert 2/3/1927 Oakland, California

Bowers, Christine Shannon, see Christine TALLEY

BOWIE, Kenneth Bernard 4/20/1960 Redwood Valley, California

Bowie, Willie Lee, see Willie Lee GRAHAM

BOWMAN, Anthony 2/7/1964 Los Angeles, California 90002

BOWMAN, Delores 9/23/1949 Los Angeles, California 90002

BOWMAN, Edna May 11/10/1930

BOWMAN, Patricia Ann 9/1/1957 Los Angeles, California 90002

BOWSER, Regina Michelle 4/1/1963 San Francisco, California

BRADSHAW, Pamela Gail 8/17/1956 Redwood Valley, California

Brady, Dorothy, see Dorothy Lee WORLEY

BRADY, Georgiann Patricia 12/23/1965 San Francisco, California

BRADY, Michaeleen Patricia 5/14/1943 San Francisco, California 94121

BRADY, Michele Margaret 12/2/1966 San Francisco, California

Brandon, Najahjuanda Jherenelle , see Najah DARNES

BREIDENBACH, Avis Jocelyn 1/5/1958

BREIDENBACH, Lois Fontaine 5/29/1928 Redwood Valley, California

BREIDENBACH, Melanie Lee 9/14/1960 Redwood Valley, California 95470

Breidenbach, Rocky, see Lois Fontaine BREIDENBACH*

BREIDENBACH, Wesley Karl 9/15/1959

BREWER, Dorothy Ann 10/24/1938 San Francisco, California

BREWSTER, Kimberly Louise 8/25/1955 San Francisco, California 94102

BRIDGEWATER, Miller 2/11/1908 Palo Alto, California 94306

Briggs, Donna Louise, see Donna Louise LACY

Bright, Babo, see Lawrence George BRIGHT, III

BRIGHT, Juanita Jean 12/8/1967 San Francisco, California

BRIGHT, Lawrence George, III 10/18/1965 San Francisco, California

BRIGHT, Ruby Jean 2/12/1947 San Francisco, California 94115

BROWN, Amanda Denise 10/13/1966

BROWN, Ava 8/6/1951 San Francisco, California

BROWN, Jerross Keith 5/8/1970

Brown, Jocelyn, see Jocelyn CARTER

BROWN, Johnny Moss, Jr. 7/19/1950

BROWN, Joyce Marie 2/8/1960 San Francisco, California 94107

BROWN, Luella Holmes 6/1/1919 Redwood Valley, California

Brown, Robert, see Robert PAUL Jr.

BROWN, Robert O. [NBC]

Brown, Ruletta, see Ruletta PAUL

BROWN, Yolanda Delaine 7/22/1963 San Francisco, California

BRYANT, Lucioes 6/23/1925 Los Angeles, California 90011

BRYANT, Princeola 10/12/1912 Los Angeles, CA 90018

BUCKLEY, Christopher Calvin 5/28/1966 San Francisco, California

BUCKLEY, Dorothy Helen 8/17/1961 San Francisco, California 94107

BUCKLEY, Frances Elizabeth 11/18/1964 San Francisco, California 94107

Buckley, Helen, see Dorothy Helen BUCKLEY

BUCKLEY, Loreatha 7/16/1957 Ukiah, California

BUCKLEY, Luna M. 5/6/1941 Ukiah, California 95482

Buckley, Minnie Luna Mae, see Luna M. BUCKLEY

BUCKLEY, Odesta 11/30/1962 San Francisco, California 94107

BURGINES, Rosie Lee 11/7/1953 Los Angeles, California 90007

Burl, Beatrice, see Beatrice Mazell JACKSON

BUSH, Billy 11/4/1964 Ukiah, California 95482

Bush, William Paul Sean, see Billy BUSH

BYRD, Bette Jean Guy 11/23/1954

C

Cain, Ruthie Mae, see Ruthie Mae QUINN

CAMERON, Beyonka Rena 10/17/1970 San Francisco, California

Camp, Lena, see Lena Mae Camp BENTON

CAMPBELL, Ronald Ray, Jr. 5/27/1972 San Francisco, California

CANADA, Mary Francis 1/20/1901 Pittsburg, California

CANNON, Thelma Doris Mattie 7/29/1930 San Francisco, California

CANNON, Vita 11/3/1962

Cannon, Vities Rochelle, see Vita CANNON

CAREY, Jeffrey James 12/12/1950 Redwood Valley, California 95482

CARR, Karen Yvette 7/18/1963 San Francisco, California 94102

Carroll, Ada, see Mildred MERCER

CARROLL, D'Artangan Angelino 8/7/1976 Berkeley, California

CARROLL, Dante 8/28/1974 Berkeley, California

CARROLL, Mickey 1/4/1973 Berkeley, California

Carroll, Mildred Ada, see Mildred MERCER

CARROLL, Randall Earl 7/16/1974 San Francisco, California

Carroll, Robert K., see Robert Keith JOHNSON

CARROLL, Rondell Jerome 8/6/1971

CARROLL, Ruby Jewell 6/10/1937

CARROLL, Wrangell Dwayne Smith 7/25/1976 San Francisco, California

CARTER, Gloria Maria 3/23/1952 Santa Barbara, California 93103

CARTER, Jocelyn 4/10/1958 San Francisco, California

CARTER, Kaywana Mae 5/10/1977 None

CARTER, Malcolm J. 8/10/1977 None

Carter, Mary Theresa, see Terry CARTER

CARTER, Maurice Chaunte 8/30/1973

Carter, Ruletta, see Ruletta PAUL

CARTER, Terry 10/3/1954 San Francisco, California

Cartmell, Patricia Ann, see Patty CARTMELL

Cartmell, Patricia Pauline, see Trisha CARTMELL

CARTMELL, Patty 7/31/1929 San Francisco, California

CARTMELL, Trisha 7/3/1954 San Francisco, California

Cartmell, Tyrone, see Tyrinia Tyrone WILLIAMS

CARTMELL, Walter Clayton 5/15/1928 Redwood Valley, California 95470

Casanova, Angelique Marie, see Angelique Marie SCHEID

Casanova, Don, see Donald Eugene SCHEID, Jr.

CASANOVA, Sophia Lauren 8/9/1967 San Francisco, California

CASTILLO, Mary Frances 1/7/1920 Los Angeles, California 90006

CASTILLO, William Richard 2/19/1944 Los Angeles, California 90006

CATNEY, Georgia Mae 10/26/1917 Redwood City, California 94061

CHACON, Stephanie Katrina 5/27/1960 Berkeley, California 94703

CHAIKIN, David Lee 1/21/1963 Redwood Valley, California 95470

Chaikin, Eugene Bernard, see Gene CHAIKIN

CHAIKIN, Gail Stephanie 2/26/1961 Redwood Valley, California

CHAIKIN, Gene 12/18/1932

CHAIKIN, Phyllis 5/6/1939 Redwood Valley, California 95470

CHAMBLISS, Jossie Evelyn 3/6/1902 San Francisco, California

CHAVIS, Loretta Diane 4/1/1955 Los Angeles, California 90007

CHRISTIAN, Robert Louis 9/10/1947 San Francisco, California 94117

CHRISTIAN, Robert Louis II 11/9/1970 San Francisco, California 94117

CHRISTIAN, Tina Rayette 9/1/1969 San Francisco, California 94117

CHRISTIAN, Vernetta Carolyn 12/25/1944 San Francisco, California 94117

Clancey, Mary Louise , see MaryLou Clancey

CLANCEY, MaryLou 4/16/1954 Redwood Valley, California

Clark , Dorothy Georgina, see Dorothy Georgina SIMPSON

CLARK, Joicy Ellis 10/28/1911 San Francisco, California 94115

CLARKE, Leola LaVerne 7/29/1909

CLAY, Nancy 5/26/1909 San Francisco, California 94117

Clayton, Janice, see Janice Arlette JOHNSON

CLIPPS, Ida Mae Pleasant 12/4/1917 San Francisco, California 94117

Coachman, Alma Coley, see Alma COLEY

Cobb, Ava, see Ava BROWN

COBB, Brenda Carole 9/4/1963 San Francisco, California

COBB, Christine 3/29/1928 San Francisco, California

Cobb, Darlene, see Darlene RAMEY

Cobb, Elois Christine, see Christine COBB

COBB, Joel Raymond 2/2/1965 San Francisco, California

Cobb, Mona, see Mona YOUNG

Cobb, Sandra Yvette , see Sandy COBB

COBB, Sandy 11/16/1956 San Francisco, California 94107

COBB, Sharon Rose 8/31/1948 Redwood Valley, California 95470

COLE, Arlander 12/22/1906 San Francisco, California

COLE, Arvella 9/28/1906 San Francisco, California

Cole, Clarence Elmer III, see Clarence KLINGMAN

Cole, Matthew Todd, see Todd KLINGMAN

Cole, William Arnold, see William KLINGMAN

COLEMAN, Mary 7/23/1894 San Francisco, California

COLEMAN, Ruth Virginia 1/3/1920 Los Angeles, California 90003

COLEY, Alma 3/10/1924 Los Angeles, California 90003

COLLINS, Susie Lee 7/20/1900 Los Angeles, California 90011

CONEDY, Inez Stricklin 3/5/1909 Palo Alto, California 94306

CONLEY, Corlis Denise 3/12/1959 11/18/1978

CONNESERO, Angela Marie 6/8/1974

COOK, Bertha Pearl 12/12/1912 Los Angeles, California 90006

COOK, Mary Ella 1/26/1914 Los Angeles, California 90006

Coomer, Loretta, see Loretta Mae CORDELL

CORDELL, Barbara Jeanne 8/14/1938 Redwood Valley, California 95470

CORDELL, Candace Kay 11/7/1960 Redwood Valley, California 95470

CORDELL, Chris Mark 9/13/1957 Redwood Valley, California 95470

CORDELL, Cindy Lyn 12/8/1959 Redwood Valley, California 95470

CORDELL, Edith Excell 2/6/1902 Redwood Valley, California 95470

CORDELL, James Joseph 10/28/1964 Redwood Valley, California 95470

Cordell, Jamie, see Jameel Regina LAWRENCE

CORDELL, Julie Rene 7/28/1961 Redwood Valley, California 95470

CORDELL, Loretta Mae 11/8/1937 Redwood Valley, California 95470

CORDELL, Mabel Joy 3/14/1962 Redwood Valley, California 95470

CORDELL, Natasha LaNa 8/17/1976

CORDELL, Richard William, Jr. 9/2/1964 San Francisco, California

CORDELL, Rita Diane 9/18/1962 San Francisco, California

Cordell, Teresa Laverne , see Shawnterri HALL

COREY, Carrie Lee 1/12/1934 San Francisco, California 94117

COREY, Ricky Anthony 9/9/1961

CORNNER, Trinidette 8/5/1970 San Francisco, California

COTTINGHAM, Mary Maide 11/30/1899 Pittsburg, California

Cox, Tanya Rena, see Tanya Rena Cox GARCIA

CRENSHAW, Eddie James 4/6/1955 San Francisco, California 94115

CRENSHAW, Francine Renita 11/21/1954 San Francisco, California 94117

CRENSHAW, Lucy 1/1/1925 San Francisco, California

CRENSHAW, Tiquan Ramon 2/26/1977

Cumer, Loretta, see Loretta Mae CORDELL

CUNNINGHAM, Millie Steans 12/25/1904 San Francisco, California 94117

D

DANIEL, Betty Leon 5/4/1951 San Francisco, California 94102

DANIEL, Steve Nathaniel III 11/18/1974

Daniels, Dorothy, see Dorothy Georgina SIMPSON

DANIELS, Michael 6/14/1964 San Francisco, California

Darden, Mary, see Mary Allie JOHNSON

Darnes, Braunshaunski, see Searcy Llewellyn DARNES

Darnes, Elondwaynion Jhontera, see Ollie B. DARNES II

DARNES, Najah 9/21/1970

Darnes, Najuandrienne, see Velma Lee DARNES

DARNES, Newhuanda Rhenelle 11/14/1959 San Francisco, California

DARNES, Ollie B., II 10/29/1967 San Francisco, California

DARNES, Searcy Llewellyn 4/21/1962 Santa Rosa, California

DARNES, Velma Lee 4/29/1936 Santa Rosa, California

DASHIELL, Hazel Frances 12/16/1899 San Francisco, California 94117

DAVIS, Barbara Marie 10/3/1925 Los Angeles, California 90007

DAVIS, Bippy 2/5/1973 San Francisco, California

Davis, Bob, see Robert Edwin DAVIS

DAVIS, Brian Andrew 7/19/1962 Burlingame, California

DAVIS, Celeste 11/21/1967 San Francisco, California

DAVIS, Cynthia Marie 12/3/1949 San Francisco, California

DAVIS, Deron Kentae 1/14/1977

DAVIS, Frances Bernadette 3/14/1928

DAVIS, Gerina Maxine 1/3/1977 San Francisco, California

DAVIS, Isabel 12/14/1906

DAVIS, Johannah Danielle 9/16/1974 San Francisco, California

DAVIS, Lexie Smith 9/22/1909 Los Angeles, California 90018

DAVIS, Margaret Virginia 1/10/1950 San Francisco, California

Davis, Margarita, see Margaret Virginia DAVIS

Davis, Michelle, see Michelle Renee WAGNER

DAVIS, Minnie Isabel 12/23/1925

DAVIS, Renee Sylvia 4/23/1971 San Francisco, California

DAVIS, Robert Edwin 4/27/1936 Ukiah, California 95482

DAWKINS, Beatrice 8/31/1918 Los Angeles, California 90018

DAWSON, Derek

DE PINA, Lovie Hattie Ann 10/18/1900 Ukiah, California 95482

DEAN, Burger Lee 11/14/1916 Los Angeles, California 90006

Dean, Virginia, see Virginia Vera TAYLOR

Dean, William Dillon , see Billy JONES

DELANEY, Edith Fredonia 12/23/1909 Ukiah, California 95482

DELIHAUSSAYES, Tammi Sherrel 9/28/1966 San Francisco, California

Dennis, Carol, see Carol Ann Cordell McCOY

DENNIS, Eddie Lee 7/4/1928 Los Angeles, California 90001

DENNIS, Ellihue 8/2/1948 San Francisco, California 94103

DENNIS, Gabriel 8/22/1968

Dennis, Leanndra, see Leanndra Renae McCOY

DENNIS, Orde 10/31/1932 Los Angeles, California 90001

Dennis, Patty, see Patty Ann McCOY

DENNIS, Ronnie 12/20/1961

Devers, Acquinetta, see Anita DEVERS

DEVERS, Anita 5/16/1954 Los Angeles, California 90001

DEVERS, Darrell Audwin 12/6/1955 Los Angeles, California 90008

DICKERSON, Roseana Eartia 3/26/1917 Richmond, California 94801

DICKSON, Bessie Lee 2/4/1914 Los Angeles, California 90001

DILLARD, Violatt Esther 9/16/1927 San Francisco, California 94102

Dixon, Bessie Lee, see Bessie Lee DICKSON

DOMINECK, Katherine Martha 10/27/1894 San Francisco, California 94121

DOUGLAS, Farene 9/10/1910 Los Angeles, California 90062

DOUGLAS, Joyce Lalar 4/3/1958 San Francisco, California

DOVER, Vicky Lynn 1/20/1958 Redwood Valley, California 95470

DOWNS, Nena Belle 4/22/1928 Los Angeles, California 90001

Duckett, Exia Marie, see Marie LAWRENCE

Duckett, Joanette Blugina, see Dee Dee LAWRENCE

Duckett, Ronald Charles , see Nicky LAWRENCE

DUNCAN, Corrie 11/6/1906 San Francisco, California 94115

DUNCAN, Ebony Latrice 7/7/1978

Duncan, Regina, see Sonja Regina DUNCAN

DUNCAN, Sonja Regina 3/29/1964 San Francisco, California

DUNCAN, Verdella 5/20/1924 San Francisco, California 94102

DUNCAN, Viola 1/13/1934 Berkeley, California 94703

Dupont, Ellen Louise, see Penny KERNS

DYSON, Florine 12/6/1890 San Francisco, California 94109

E

EDDINS, Irene 1/4/1902 San Francisco, California 94119

EDWARDS, Irene 7/23/1921 San Francisco, California 94119

EDWARDS, Isaac, Jr. 6/9/1972 San Francisco, California

EDWARDS, James 11/28/1920

Edwards, Reb, see James EDWARDS

Edwards, Rev., see James EDWARDS

EDWARDS, Shirley Ann 12/14/1951 San Francisco, California 94117

EDWARDS, Zipporah 5/27/1905 San Francisco, California 94117

EICHLER, Erin Jahna 3/13/1960 Redwood Valley, California 95470

EICHLER, Evelyn Marie 8/19/1955 Redwood Valley, California 95470

Eichler, Laetitia Marie, see Tish LeROY

Ellen, Kerns, see Penny KERNS

EVER REJOICING, 10/9/1881 Redwood Valley, California

F

FAIN, Tinetra La Dese 11/8/1958 Los Angeles, California 90008

FAIR, Amanda 12/10/1908 San Francisco, California 94121

FAIR, Sylvester Clarence 3/9/1908 San Francisco, California 94117

FARRELL, Barbara Louise 10/5/1933 San Francisco, California 94115

FARRIS, Marshall 8/5/1907 San Francisco, California 94124

FELTON, Michael Donnell 10/1/1973

FIELDS, James Donald 6/4/1932 Northridge, California 91324

FIELDS, Lori Beth 12/6/1965 Northridge, California 91324

FIELDS, Mark Evan 3/22/1967 Northridge, California 91324

FIELDS, Shirley Ann 12/15/1937 Northridge, California 91324

FINLEY, Felawnta Tyece 3/17/1969

FINLEY, Lucretia Yvette 1/19/1967

FINNEY, Casey Nakyia 7/15/1959 Los Angeles, California 90047

FITCH, Betty Jean 6/2/1955 San Francisco, California 94117

FITCH, Dawnyelle 9/4/1974 San Francisco, California

FITCH, Donald Kirk 4/15/1946 Redwood Valley, California

FITCH, Maureen Cynthia 6/13/1949 Ukiah, California 95482

Fitch, Michelle, see Michelle Renee WAGNER

FITCH, Raymond Xavier 9/11/1976 San Francisco, California

FITCH, Thomas Ray 5/17/1949 San Francisco, California

FLOWERS, Rebecca Ann 7/7/1953 San Francisco, California 94115

FONZELLE, Toi 1/17/1955 Los Angeles, California 90011

Ford, Anita, see Helen LOVE

FORD, Anthony Lamar 4/16/1963 San Francisco, California

FORD, Edward Lee 6/23/1965 San Francisco, California

FORD, Fannie 1/9/1934 Los Angeles, California 90037

Ford, Helen, see Helen LOVE

Ford, James E., see James WADE

FORD, Mary Lee 11/2/1929 Los Angeles, California

FORKS, George 3/2/1970 San Francisco, California

Forks, Viola Duncan, see Viola DUNCAN

Fortson, Hue Ishi Jr., see Ishi FORTSON

FORTSON, Ishi 9/22/1974 Los Angeles, California

FORTSON, Rhonda Denise 8/26/1954 Los Angeles, California 90011

FOSTER, Beulah 9/14/1903 Los Angeles, California 90006

FOUNTAIN, Betty Jewel 8/14/1949 Los Angeles, California 90003

FOUNTAIN, Frankie Jay 4/19/1973

FOUNTAIN, Jewel Lynn 4/11/1974

FRANKLIN, Christopher Darnnell 12/30/1975

Franklin, Jackie, see Jackie ROCHELLE

FRANKLIN, Laketta Lashun 10/7/1970

FRANKLIN, Robert Eddie Lee, Jr. 6/17/1958 Oakland, California 94608

FROHM, Connie 2/9/1955 Redwood Valley, California 95470

Frohm, Constance B. , see Connie FROHM

FULTON, Shiron 3/31/1967

FYE, Kimberly Ann 12/10/1959 Ukiah, California 95482

G

GALLIE, Bof William 10/22/1973 Redwood Valley, California 95470

Garcia, Avis, see Avis Jocelyn BREIDENBACH

GARCIA, Cleveland Desmond 5/26/1960 Los Angeles, California

GARCIA, Mary Helen 9/19/1938 Los Angeles, California

GARCIA, Susan 11/16/1962

GARCIA, Tanya Rena Cox 9/10/1958

GARCIA, Tiffany La Trice 12/21/1974 San Francisco, California

GARDENER, John Lawrence 9/20/1960 Ukiah, California 95482

GARDFREY, Danielle 8/2/1965 San Francisco, California

GARDFREY, Dominique 4/21/1968 San Francisco, California

GARDFREY, Kenneth Darren 1/29/1971 San Francisco, California

GAYLOR, Shonda Marie 6/17/1968 San Francisco, California

GEE, Herman W. 3/27/1897 Oakland, California 94606

GEORGE, David

GEORGE, Gabrielle

GEORGE, Philip

GERNANDT, Eugenia 3/12/1923 San Francisco, California

GIBSON, Mattie 12/24/1905 San Francisco, California 94115

GIEG, Jason 1/21/1975 San Francisco, California 94115

GIEG, Renee Elaine 6/9/1955 San Francisco, California 94115

GIEG, Robert Wendell 7/25/1951 San Francisco, California 94115

Gieg, Romaldo, see Romaldo Benjamin HICKS

Gieg, Shirley, see Shirley Pat HICKS

GIEG, Stanley Brian 1/20/1959 San Francisco, California 94115

Gilbert, MN, see Jerry Gilbert SMITH

GILL, Betty Jean 7/16/1960 San Francisco, California

GILL, Irma Lee 2/5/1912 San Francisco, California

GILL, Jimmy 11/14/1962

GODSHALK, Viola May 2/10/1921 Redwood Valley, California

Gomez, Harry, see Henry Lee LOGAN

GOMEZ, Wanda Denise 8/1/1972

GOODSPEED, Claude 6/13/1905 Los Angeles, California 90044

GOODSPEED, Lue Dimple 1/3/1907 Los Angeles, California 90044

GOODWIN, David Lee 8/28/1965

GOSNEY, Mark Hartley 11/28/1973 Redwood Valley, California 95470

GRADY, Willie James 7/4/1954 Los Angeles, California 90006

Graham, Kathryn, see Kathryn Denise JACKSON

GRAHAM, Willie Lee 2/9/1907 Los Angeles, California 90001

Grauman, Kathryn, see Kathryn Denise JACKSON

Green, Darrell see Darrell MARTIN

GREEN, Juanita 9/5/1916 Oakland, California 94602

GREENE, Anitra Rochelle 1/8/1961 Los Angeles, California 90003

GRIFFITH, Amondo 3/10/1960 San Francisco, California 94124

GRIFFITH, Camella 10/29/1977

GRIFFITH, Emmett Alexander, Jr. 7/11/1958 Redwood Valley, California

Griffith, Gloria, see Gloria Faye WARREN

GRIFFITH, Mae Kathryn 12/26/1941 Los Angeles, California 90037

GRIFFITH, Marrian Louise 9/13/1961

GRIFFITH, Mary Magdaline 1/28/1927 San Francisco, California

GRIGSBY, Frankie Lee 5/17/1926 San Francisco, California

GRIMM, Ronald Windus 1/16/1937 San Rafael, California 94901

GRIMM, Sue L. 3/4/1941 San Rafael, California 94901

GRIMM, Tina Lynn 5/9/1960 San Rafael, California 94901

Grissette, Barbara, see Barbara Ann SMITH

GRISSETTE, Youlanda 6/15/1966 San Francisco, California

GROOT, Pauline 5/30/1950 Santa Rosa, California 95401

GRUBBS, Clark 1/17/1967

Grubbs, Gerald Richard, see Ken NORTON

GRUBBS, Kelly 1/14/1964 San Francisco, California

Grubbs, Kevan, see Kevin GRUBBS

GRUBBS, Kevin 5/21/1961 Ukiah, California 95482

Grubbs, Lemuel Thomas II, see Tom GRUBBS

GRUBBS, Sylvia Elaine 11/10/1938 Ukiah, California

GRUBBS, Tom 11/20/1941 Los Angeles, California 90006

GRUNNETT, Patricia Lee 11/25/1941 Redwood Valley, California 95470

GUIDRY, Mercedese Mavis Clare 9/6/1908 Los Angeles, California 90006

GURVICH, Jann Elizabeth 11/5/1953 Berkeley, California 94702

GUY, Brian 9/8/1966 San Francisco, California 94134

Guy, Cody, see Betty Jean Guy BYRD

GUY, Keith Le Jon 9/12/1967 San Francisco, California 94134

GUY, Kimberley Denee 7/29/1971 San Francisco, California 94134

GUY, Ottie Mese 6/8/1944 San Francisco, California 94134

GUY, Sharitta Renae 2/12/1974 San Francisco, California 94134

GUY, Thurman, III 12/2/1962 San Francisco, California 94134

H

HALKMAN, Rochelle Dawanna 9/30/1952 San Francisco, California 94117

HALL, Carl Glouster 3/16/1904 Los Angeles, California 90019

HALL, Heloise Janice 12/7/1911 Los Angeles, California 90019

HALL, Shawnterri 3/11/1958 San Francisco, California 94115

Hallmon, Eddie James, see Eddie James CRENSHAW

Hallmon, Francine, see Francine Renita CRENSHAW

Hallmon, Tiquan Ramon , see Tiquan Ramon CRENSHAW

Hanley, Hassan Ali, see Hassan SMITH

HARMS, Karen Marie 6/14/1958 Ukiah, California

HARPER, Artee 1/28/1910 Los Angeles, California 90003

Harrell, Joanette, see Dee Dee LAWRENCE

HARRINGTON, Ollie B. 11/7/1940 Los Angeles, California 90003

HARRIS, Annie Mae 1/22/1904 Los Angeles, California 90003

HARRIS, Constance 11/27/1932 Ukiah, California 95482

Harris, Constance Nicole, see Constance HARRIS

HARRIS, Donald

Harris, Dorothy Lasheen, see Dottie HARRIS

HARRIS, Dottie 1/17/1961 Ukiah, California

HARRIS, John 7/31/1932 Oakland, California

HARRIS, Josephine 12/24/1907 Los Angeles, California

HARRIS, Liane 11/27/1956 Redwood Valley, California 95470

Harris, Linda Sharon, see Sharon AMOS

HARRIS, Magnolia Costella 12/11/1916 San Francisco, California 94117

HARRIS, Nevada 1/21/1910 Los Angeles, California 90006

Harris, Shajhuanna Lesheene, see Dottie HARRIS

Harris, Willie Maude , see Constance HARRIS

Hayden, Eyvonne Paris, see Eyvonne JAMES

HEATH, Florence 5/8/1928 Pittsburg, California 94565

HEATH, Michael DiAngelo 4/25/1964 Pittsburg, California 94565

HELLE, Joseph Leo III 6/6/1950 San Francisco, California 94115

HENDERSON, Beatrice 8/22/1903 San Francisco, California 94117

Henderson, Charles Douglas , see Chuckie HENDERSON

HENDERSON, Charles Garry 9/11/1978

HENDERSON, Chuckie 3/8/1960

HENDERSON, Kenya Lakiah 7/27/1977 San Francisco, California

Henderson, Mattie B., see Beatrice HENDERSON

Henderson, Pat, see Patricia Ann BOWMAN

Hennley, Hassan Ali, see Hassan SMITH

HERRING, Nena Davidson 1/15/1906 San Francisco, California 90001

HICKS, Anthony Allan 3/4/1966 San Francisco, California

HICKS, Marthea Ann 5/22/1935 San Francisco, California 94121

HICKS, Romaldo Benjamin 11/6/1965 San Francisco, California

HICKS, Shirley Pat 3/14/1943 San Francisco, California

HILL, Emma Mae 12/5/1915 Los Angeles, California 90001

HILTON, Osialee 1/4/1894 Los Angeles, California 90001

HINES, Bernell Maurice 8/12/1914 San Bruno, California 94066

HINES, Mable Ellen Walker 12/29/1912

HINES, Rosa Mae 9/25/1908 Los Angeles, California 90006

HOLLEY, Patricia Ann 11/18/1957 San Francisco, California 94115

HOLLIDAY, Tanai Claudine-La Dese 3/17/1976

Holmes, Luella, see Luella Holmes BROWN

Holmes, Peter, see John HARRIS

HORNE, Hazel Lark 6/20/1915 Los Angeles, California 90011

HOUSTON, Judy Lynn 11/9/1964 San Francisco, California 94107

HOUSTON, Patricia Dian 10/2/1963 San Francisco, California 94107

HOUSTON, Phyllis Dian 3/26/1944 Ukiah, California 95482

HOWARD, Dorris Hellen 1/27/1922 Oakland, California

Howard, Exia Marie, see Marie LAWRENCE

HOYER, Barbara Faye 9/21/1948 San Francisco, California 94115

Hunter, Denise, see Denise Elaine PURIFOY

Hunter, Rose, see Rose Jeanette SHELTON

I

Ijames, Anita, see Anita Christine KELLEY

IJAMES, Judith Kay 12/6/1949 Calpella, California 95418

IJAMES, Maya Lisa 9/8/1969 San Francisco, California

INGHRAM, Alice Lorine 9/24/1936 Redwood Valley, California 95470

INGHRAM, Ava Jillon 7/25/1963 Redwood Valley, California 95470

Ingram, Candace, see Candace Kay CORDELL

J

Jackson, "Mom", see Luvenia JACKSON

JACKSON, Beatrice Alberta 12/22/1896 San Francisco, California 94115

JACKSON, Beatrice Mazell Los Angeles, California

Jackson, Clarence, see Clarence KLINGMAN

Jackson, Corrine Mae, see Rennie KICE

Jackson, Darrell D. Martin, see Darrell MARTIN

JACKSON, David Bettis 12/1/1892 Los Angeles, California

JACKSON, Donald 7/13/1944 San Francisco, California 94102

Jackson, Ebony, see Ebony Latrice DUNCAN

JACKSON, Eileen Renee 6/2/1965 Redwood Valley, California 95470

JACKSON, Gladys Margarette 7/6/1919 Los Angeles, California 90007

JACKSON, Jonathan 5/7/1978

JACKSON, Kathryn Denise 9/24/1952 Fremont, California

Jackson, Kathy, see Kathryn Denise JACKSON

JACKSON, Leticia 2/9/1970 San Francisco, California 94115

JACKSON, Lourece 12/26/1941 San Francisco, California 94112

JACKSON, Luvenia 7/5/1897 Los Angeles, California

JACKSON, Paulette Karen 2/17/1951 San Francisco, California 94117

Jackson, Pop, see David Bettis JACKSON

JACKSON, Ralph Edwin 6/9/1952 Fremont, California

Jackson, Rennie, see Rennie KICE

JACKSON, Richard Stuart 5/22/1973 San Francisco, California 94112

JACKSON, Rosa Lee 10/21/1939 San Francisco, California 94115

JACKSON, Thelma 8/27/1936 San Francisco, California 94102

JAMES, Eyvonne 9/8/1959 San Francisco, California 94102

JAMES, Lavana 2/26/1904 Los Angeles, California 90001

JAMES, Margaret 2/27/1918 San Francisco, California

JAMES, Ronald DeVal 11/1/1955 San Francisco, California 94117

James, Shanda Michelle, see Shanda Michelle OLIVER

JAMES, Toni Denise 7/21/1959 Los Angeles, California 90011

JANARO, Daren Richard 5/1/1964 Redwood Valley, California 95470

JANARO, Marvin 4/9/1963

JANARO, Mauri Kay 11/20/1962 Redwood Valley, California 95470

JEFFERY, Eartis 2/18/1913 Los Angeles, California 90037

JEFFERY, Margrette 9/4/1913 Los Angeles, California 90037

Jensen, Debby, see Deborah Faye SCHROEDER

Jensen, Tad, see Tad SCHROEDER

Jerram, Susan Jane, see Susan NOXON

JOHNSON, Berda Truss 4/2/1892 Los Angeles, California 90007

JOHNSON, Bessie Marie Jance 3/26/1936 San Francisco, California 94117

Johnson, Bette Jean, see Betty Jean Guy BYRD

Johnson, Birdie, see Berda Truss JOHNSON

JOHNSON, Carman Lisa 7/25/1968 San Francisco, California

JOHNSON, Clara LaNue 11/24/1932 Los Angeles, California 90008

Johnson, Cody, see Betty Jean Guy BYRD

JOHNSON, Denise 10/25/1961 San Francisco, California

JOHNSON, Derek Damone 2/21/1970 San Francisco, California 94115

JOHNSON, Deshon 2/26/1973 San Francisco, California

JOHNSON, Earl Luches Joseph 1/2/1912 Los Angeles, California

JOHNSON, Garnett Blake 11/30/1963

Johnson, Garry Dartez, see Poncho JOHNSON

JOHNSON, Gerald Duane 1/17/1961 Los Angeles, California 90037

JOHNSON, Gleniel 6/1/1971

JOHNSON, Gwendolyn Joyce 2/19/1962 San Francisco, California

JOHNSON, Helen 11/25/1927 Los Angeles, California

JOHNSON, Irra Jean 7/8/1952 San Francisco, California 94115

JOHNSON, James Douglas 6/22/1962

JOHNSON, Janice Arlette* 5/29/1960 Los Angeles, California 90008

JOHNSON, Jessie A. 9/17/1900 Los Angeles, California 90001

JOHNSON, Joe, Jr. 7/12/1957 San Francisco, California

JOHNSON, Koya Tynsia 6/5/1976

JOHNSON, Mahaley 6/5/1910 Los Angeles, California 90037

JOHNSON, Maisha Danika 12/28/1976

Johnson, Mary Alice, see Mary Allie JOHNSON

JOHNSON, Mary Allie 2/22/1947 San Francisco, California

JOHNSON, Mary E. 10/20/1927

JOHNSON, Naomi Esther 10/15/1928 San Francisco, California 94115

JOHNSON, Patsy Ruth 8/3/1950 San Francisco, California

JOHNSON, Poncho 10/5/1959

Johnson, Richard Lee, see Ricky JOHNSON

JOHNSON, Ricky 8/3/1958 Daly City, California 94014

JOHNSON, Robert 12/8/1903 Ukiah, California 95482

JOHNSON, Robert Keith 4/2/1966 Los Angeles, California

JOHNSON, Ruby Lee 12/16/1921 San Francisco, California 94112

JOHNSON, Saleata Lateais 8/22/1969 San Francisco, California

JOHNSON, Samuel Lee 5/5/1952 Richmond, California

Johnson, Sharon Denise, see Denise JOHNSON

JOHNSON, Shawntiki 11/30/1958 San Francisco, California

Johnson, Shiron, see Shiron FULTON

JOHNSON, Thomas William 11/8/1956

Johnson, Tinetra, see Tinetra La Dese FAIN

Johnson, Verna Lisa, see Shawntiki JOHNSON

JOHNSON, Willa JoAnn 5/22/1959 Los Angeles, California 90008

JONES, Addie B. 8/18/1908

Jones, Adeline, see Addie B. JONES

JONES, Agnes Paulette 2/14/1943 San Francisco, California

JONES, Annette Teresa 2/25/1926 Los Angeles, California 90018

Jones, Ava Phenice, see Ava BROWN

Jones, Barbara, see Barbara Alberta KEMP

Jones, Billie, see Billy JONES

JONES, Billy 8/30/1961

JONES, Brenda Yvonne 12/13/1948 San Francisco, California 94107

JONES, Chaeoke Warren 4/4/1977 none

Jones, Constance Harris, see Constance HARRIS

Jones, Darlene, see Darlene RAMEY

JONES, Earnest 9/7/1922 Los Angeles, California

JONES, Eliza 6/25/1910 Ukiah, California 95482

JONES, Forrest Ray 12/12/1936 Ukiah, California

JONES, James Warren (Rev.) 5/13/1931 Redwood Valley, California 95470

JONES, Jessie Weana 5/3/1924 Los Angeles, California 90001

Jones, Jim Arthur, see Jimbo JONES

JONES, Jimbo 11/25/1964 San Francisco, California 94107

Jones, Johnny Moss, see Johnny Moss BROWN, Jr.

JONES, Kwame Rhu Amarka 9/3/1968 San Francisco, California

JONES, Larry Darnell 1/14/1953 San Francisco, California 94115

JONES, Lerna Veshaun 1/19/1969 San Francisco, California 94107

JONES, Lew Eric 11/23/1956 Redwood Valley, California 95470

JONES, Marceline Mae Baldwin 1/8/1927 Redwood Valley, California 95470

JONES, Marchelle Jacole 2/14/1978

Jones, Mary Theresa, see Terry CARTER

JONES, Michael Ray 6/7/1971

JONES, Monyelle Maylene 2/14/1978

JONES, Nancy Mae 5/5/1901 Pittsburg, California 94565

Jones, Sandy, see Sandy COBB

Jones, Sharon, see Sharon Rose COBB

JONES, Stephanie 12/20/1963 San Francisco, California

Jones, Terry Carter, see Terry CARTER

Jones, Tim "Night", see Timothy Borl JONES

JONES, Timothy Borl 6/3/1959

Jones, Toni, see Toni Denise JAMES

JONES, Valerie Yvette 11/20/1958 San Francisco, California

JONES, Vellersteane 9/3/1926 San Francisco, California

JORDAN, Dessie Jones 6/1/1908 San Francisco, California 94115

JORDAN, Fannie Alberta 8/6/1913 Los Angeles, California 90044

JORDAN, Lula Elizabeth 11/25/1907 San Francisco, California

JOY, Love Madgeleane 12/18/1891 San Francisco, California

JURADO, Emma Jane 12/20/1908 San Francisco, California 94117

K

KATSARIS, Maria 6/9/1953 Redwood Valley, California 95470

KEATON, Rosa Lorenda Mae 2/20/1907 Los Angeles, California 90011

KEATON, Tommie Sheppard, Sr. 8/12/1914 Los Angeles, California 90011

Keeler, Elaine Roslyn, see Pat KEELER

KEELER, Pat 5/8/1944 San Francisco, California

KELLER, Darell Eugene 7/21/1949 Oakland, California 94609

KELLEY, Anita Christine 3/15/1950 Ukiah, California 95482

KELLEY, Viola B. 12/13/1906 Redwood City, California 94063

Kelly, Paulette, see Paulette Karen JACKSON

KEMP, Barbara Alberta 11/4/1941 Ukiah, California 95482

KEMP, Mellonie Denise 8/13/1964 Ukiah, California 95482

KEMP, Rochelle Annette 4/28/1968 Ukiah, California 95482

KENDALL, Elfreida 10/30/1909 Los Angeles, California

KENNEDY, Emma Addie 10/28/1911 Los Angeles, California 90008

KERNS, Carol Ann 4/28/1958 San Francisco, California

Kerns, Ellen, see Penny KERNS

KERNS, Penny 11/13/1930 Los Angeles, California 90006

KICE, Bob 1/4/1948 Redwood Valley, California 95470

Kice, Corrine, see Rennie KICE

KICE, Rennie 3/11/1945 Redwood Valley, California 95470

Kice, Robert Edward , see Bob KICE

KICE, Thomas David, 2nd 1/14/1966 Redwood Valley, California 95470

KICE, Thomas David, Sr. 11/18/1935 Redwood Valley, California 95470

KING, Charlotte 10/26/1897 San Francisco, California 94109

KING, Leola 4/2/1913 San Francisco, California 94115

KING, Teresa Lynn 1/11/1947 San Francisco, California 94107

KING, Wanda Bonita 7/14/1939 Ukiah, California 95482

Kirkendall, Carolyn, see Carolyn Ann THOMAS

KISLINGBURY, Sharon Jean 10/16/1956 San Francisco, California

KLINGMAN, April Heather 4/5/1973 San Francisco, California

KLINGMAN, Clarence 8/11/1963 Ukiah, California 95482

KLINGMAN, Martha Ellen 5/9/1946 Ukiah, California 95482

KLINGMAN, Todd 11/12/1967 San Francisco, California

KLINGMAN, William 1/13/1965 San Francisco, California

Knox, James Douglas, see James Douglas JOHNSON

KUTULAS, Dan 2/20/1927 Redwood Valley, California 95470

Kutulas, Demosthenis, see Dan KUTULAS

KUTULAS, Edith 12/8/1929 Redwood Valley, California 95470

L

LACY, Donna Louise 11/15/1962 Redwood Valley, California

LACY, Georgia Lee 2/9/1910 Redwood Valley, California 95470

LACY, Tony Linton 2/10/1964 San Francisco, California

Lamotha, Ramona, see Mona YOUNG

LAND, Pearl 7/29/1902 San Francisco, California 94102

Lang, Judy Kay, see Judith Kay IJAMES

LANG, Lossie Mae 2/16/1904 San Francisco, California

LANGSTON, Carrie Ola 2/10/1923 Richmond, California 94801

LANGSTON, Marianita 12/10/1955 Richmond, California 94801

LANGSTON, Zuretti Jenicer 7/25/1959 Richmond, California 94801

LAWRENCE, Dee Dee 12/31/1963 San Francisco, California 94107

Lawrence, Erin, see Erin Jahna EICHLER

LAWRENCE, Jameel Regina 5/12/1973

LAWRENCE, Marie 1/20/1945 San Francisco, California

LAWRENCE, Nawab 11/20/1967

LAWRENCE, Nicky 10/14/1962 San Francisco, California 94107

LAYTON, Carolyn Louise Moore 7/13/1945 San Francisco, California

LAYTON, Karen Lea Tow 8/10/1947 Ukiah, California 95482

Layton, Kimo, see Jim Jon (Kimo) PROKES

LEE, Daisy 12/5/1956 San Francisco, California 94133

LENDO, Karen Marie 10/15/1960 San Francisco, California 94115

Lenin, Janet, see Janet Marie TUPPER

Lenin, Mary, see Mary Elizabeth TUPPER

LeRoy, Erin, see Erin Jahna EICHLER

LeRoy, Evelyn Marie, see Evelyn Marie EICHLER

LeRoy, Letitia Marie, see Tish LeROY

LeROY, Tish 9/14/1930 San Francisco, California

LEWIS, Adrienne Rochan 7/10/1966 San Francisco, California

LEWIS, Alecha Julianne 8/23/1969 San Francisco, California

LEWIS, Barry Eugene 7/4/1964 San Francisco, California

LEWIS, Casandra Florene 9/8/1970 San Francisco, California

LEWIS, Dana Michelle 3/25/1970 San Francisco, California

LEWIS, Doris Jane 10/12/1940 San Francisco, California

Lewis, Dorsey J. , see Doris Jane LEWIS

LEWIS, Freddie Lee, Jr. 2/27/1963 San Francisco, California

LEWIS, Karen 10/23/1959 San Francisco, California

LEWIS, Lisa Michelle 2/2/1962 San Francisco, California 94115

LEWIS, Lue Ester 4/21/1930 Los Angeles, California 90002

Linton, Tommy Oscar, Jr., see Tony Linton LACY

Linton, Tony, see Tony Linton LACY

LIVINGSTON, Beverly Marie Geraldine 4/15/1932 Ukiah, California 95482

LIVINGSTON, Jerry Dwight 11/11/1941 Ukiah, California 95482

LOCKETT, Gordon Evrette 9/23/1918 Oakland, California 94607

LOGAN, Henry Lee 9/12/1938

LOOMAN, Carolyn Sue 5/7/1943 San Francisco, California 94115

LOPEZ, Vincent, Jr. 2/26/1963

Love, Heavenly, see Helen LOVE

LOVE, Helen 11/6/1900 San Francisco, California

LOVE, Mary

LOWE, Love Life Georgia Belle 12/2/1888 Redwood Valley, California

LOWERY, Ruth Whiteside 4/26/1921 Los Angeles, California 90043

LUCAS, Lovie Jean Morton 11/16/1903 San Francisco, California

LUCIENTIES, Christine Renee 1/22/1952 Ukiah, California 95482

Lund, Chris, see Christian Leo ROZYNKO

Lund, Joyce, see Joyce ROZYNKO

Lund, Mike, see Michael Thomas ROZYNKO

LUNDQUIST, Diane 12/31/1946 San Francisco, California 94117

LUNDQUIST, Dov Mario 3/29/1967 Redwood Valley, California 95470

Lundquist, Jemal, see Jemeal PATTERSON

LYLES, Minnie Magaline 2/28/1928 San Francisco, California 94109

M

MACON, Dee Dee 7/17/1945 Redwood Valley, California 95470

Macon, Dorothy, see Dee Dee MACON

MALLOY, Lillian 8/10/1905 San Francisco, California

MALONE, Willie 11/14/1963 San Francisco, California

MARCH, Alfred Shellie II 9/10/1964

MARCH, Alfreda Suzette 9/10/1964

MARCH, Anita Elaine 1/14/1962

MARCH, Earnestine Thomas 6/29/1930 San Francisco, California 94110

MARSHALL, Charles 2/16/1957 San Francisco, California 94132

MARSHALL, Danny Leon 12/24/1954 San Francisco, California 94132

MARSHALL, Diana LaVerne 2/28/1959 San Francisco, California 94132

MARSHALL, Shaunte 4/11/1978 none

Marshall, Vicky Lynn, see Vicky Lynn DOVER

Martin, Bessie, see Bessie Marie Jance JOHNSON

MARTIN, Darrell 1/6/1965 San Francisco, California

Mason, Diane, see Diana McKNIGHT

Mason, Francine Renita, see Francine Renita CRENSHAW

MASON, Irene 11/15/1892 Los Angeles, California

MAYSHACK, Mary 7/20/1905

McCALL, Cheryle Darnell 12/31/1947 San Francisco, California

McCALL, Donald Wayne 11/18/1966 San Francisco, California

McCALL, Estelle Dunn 10/7/1930 San Francisco, California

McCann, Bea, see Beatrice Claudine BELL

McCANN, Danny 2/24/1975 San Francisco, California

McCANN, Eileen Kelly 1/28/1960 San Francisco, California 94117

McCANN, Maria Louise 10/27/1952 San Francisco, California

McCANN, Michael Angelo 4/6/1974

McCANN, Rori 5/2/1973

McCann, Rori Lynette, see Rori McCANN

McCLAIN, Allie 6/25/1890 Los Angeles, California

McCOY, Carol Ann Cordell 9/9/1945 Redwood Valley, California 95470

McCOY, Leanndra Renae 2/16/1969 Redwood Valley, California

McCOY, Lowell Francis, 2nd 8/18/1966 San Francisco, California

McCOY, Marcenda Dyann 10/16/1970 Redwood Valley, California

McCOY, Patty Ann 10/6/1964 Redwood Valley, California

McELVANE, James Nelson 4/13/1932 Ukiah, California 95482

McGOWAN, Alluvine 3/13/1888 San Francisco, California 94117

McGOWAN, Annie Jane 4/6/1908 Redwood Valley, California 95470

McINTYRE, Joyce Faye 10/23/1957 San Francisco, California

McKENZIE, Clara L. 11/26/1929 San Francisco, California

McKINNIS, Levatus V. 7/1/1906 Berkeley, California

McKNIGHT, Diana 9/9/1956 Oakland, California 94607

McKNIGHT, Earl 2/18/1895 San Francisco, California 94117

McKNIGHT, Ray Anthony 10/12/1955

McKNIGHT, Raymond Anthony 6/1/1975 Oakland, California

McKNIGHT, Rose Marie 8/23/1953 Oakland, California 94607

McMURRY, Deidre Renee 1/22/1961 Berkeley, California 94703

McMurry, Eileen, see Eileen Kelly McCANN

McMURRY, Sebastian R.C. 3/2/1955 Berkeley, California

McMURRY, Takiyah Chane 3/12/1978 none

McMURRY, Teddy 6/7/1958 Oakland, California 94609

McMurry, Theodore Devanulis, see Teddy McMURRY

McNEAL, Jessie Belle 6/19/1910 Los Angeles, California 90011

MERCER, Henry 4/3/1902 San Francisco, California 94119

MERCER, Mildred 2/19/1899 San Francisco, California 94109

MIDDLETON, Virginia 10/25/1915 San Francisco, California

MILLER, Christine 6/4/1918 Los Angeles, California 90005

MILLER, Lucy Jane 3/31/1913 San Francisco, California

MINOR, Cassandra Yvette 10/15/1956 Redwood Valley, California 95470

MINOR, Cuyana Lynette 4/30/1978 none

MITCHELL, Annie Lee 7/7/1930 Los Angeles, California 90011

MITCHELL, Beverly Ann 1/19/1943 San Francisco, California

MITCHELL, Beverly Darlene 11/14/1962 Los Angeles, California 90011

MITCHELL, Callie Mae 3/25/1913 San Francisco, California

MITCHELL, Lawanda Jean 3/6/1964

MITCHELL, Lee Charles (L.C.) 7/24/1931 Los Angeles, California 90011

Mitchell, Otis, see Ben ROBINSON

MITCHELL, Shirley Ann 3/9/1957 San Francisco, California 94115

MITCHELL, Tony Lavell 8/15/1965 Los Angeles, California 90011

MOORE, Ann Elizabeth 5/12/1954 San Francisco, California

MOORE, Betty Karen 4/26/1950 San Francisco, California

Moore, Billy, see William Allan WATKINS

Moore, Clarence Edward, Jr., see Clarence ARTERBERRY

MOORE, Edward 8/26/1915 Los Angeles, California 90019

MOREHEAD, Leola Kennedy 2/26/1926 Oakland, California 94605

Morgan, Lydia, see Lydia ATKINS

MORGAN, Marcus Emile 12/5/1970

MORGAN, Oliver, Jr. 9/5/1949 La Palma, California 90623

Morrel, Luna, see Luna M. BUCKLEY

MORRIS, Pearley 1/29/1912 San Francisco, California

MORRISON, Erris Andrew 3/13/1963 San Francisco, California

MORRISON, Lugenia 6/22/1927 Los Angeles, California 90059

MORRISON, Yvonne 10/12/1959 Los Angeles, California 90059

MORTON, Mary Nathaniel 1/24/1942 Pittsburg, California 94565

MORTON, Vickie 2/7/1970 Pittsburg, California

MOSES, Eura Lee 9/12/1899 Los Angeles, California 90003

MOTON, Danny McCarter 12/2/1956 San Francisco, California

Moton, Deanna Kay, see Deanna (Diane) (Diana) Kay WILKINSON

MOTON, Glen 10/11/1910 San Francisco, California

MOTON, Michael Javonnie 4/15/1973 San Francisco, California

Moton, Pamela, see Pamela Gail BRADSHAW

MOTON, Russell DeAndrea 3/2/1948 Los Angeles, California

MOTON, Viola Mae 11/7/1920 Pomona, California 91766

MUELLER, Esther Lillian 3/30/1902 Redwood Valley, California 95470

MULDROW, Yvette Louise 10/23/1958 San Francisco, California 94124

MURPHY, Lela Loenma 7/17/1897

MURPHY, Mary E. 1/8/1898 San Francisco, California

MURRAY, Detra Renee 4/13/1968 San Francisco, California

MUTSCHMANN, Jane Ellen 12/27/1947 San Francisco, California

N

NAILOR, Gertrude 3/21/1910 Pasadena, California 91103

NEAL, Cardell 12/17/1954 San Francisco, California

Neal, Marilee, see Marilee Faith BOGUE

Nelson, Enola Marthenya, see Kay NELSON

NELSON, Kay 12/9/1920 Los Angeles, California 90008

NEWELL, Allen 7/25/1964 San Francisco, California

Newell, Ann, see Shirley Ann EDWARDS

NEWELL, Christopher 7/10/1961 Los Angeles, California 90002

NEWELL, Hazle Maria 6/15/1927 Los Angeles, California 90002

NEWELL, Jennifer 1/13/1967

NEWELL, Karl 11/13/1962

NEWELL, Shirley 12/24/1955 Los Angeles, California 90019

NEWMAN, Darlene Rudeltha 3/12/1948 San Francisco, California 94117

Newman, Kenya, see Kenya Lakiah HENDERSON

NEWMAN, Lonnie Alexander 1/11/1973 San Francisco, California

NEWMAN, Luigi Lemoyne 3/7/1969 San Francisco, California

NEWSOME, Benjamin Keith 10/28/1964 San Francisco, California

NICHOLS, Ida May 7/31/1900 Los Angeles, California 90006

Norris, Claudia Jo, see Claudia Jo BOUQUET

NORTON, Ken 2/15/1945 Los Angeles, California 90006

NORWOOD, Fairy Lee 1/27/1930 San Francisco, California 94117

NOXON, Susan 4/25/1945 San Francisco, California 94115

O

O'BRYANT, Winnieann Zelline 2/2/1899 Redwood Valley, California

O'Bryant, Zelline, see Winnieann Zelline O'BRYANT

O'Neal, Benjamin, see Ben ROBINSON

OLIVER, Bruce Howard 3/18/1958 San Francisco, California 94115

OLIVER, Shanda Michelle 4/4/1959 San Francisco, California 94117

OLIVER, William Sheldon 12/25/1959 San Francisco, California 94115

Owens, Georgia, see Love Life Georgia Belle LOWE

OWENS, Jane Elizabeth 11/14/1920 San Francisco, California 94117

Owens, Michkell Paniel , see Mickey CARROLL

P

PAGE, Rhonda Rachelle 2/10/1954 Oakland, California 94609

PARKER, Beatrice Lucy 8/27/1894 San Francisco, California 94109

Parker, Bethany Shawnee, see Shawn WALKER

Parker, Cheryle Darnell, see Cheryle Darnell McCALL

Parker, Gloria Victoria, see Vickie Morton

PARKS, J. Warren 9/2/1973 San Francisco, California

PARKS, Patty Lou 4/29/1934 Ukiah, California 95482

PARRIS, Lore Bee 2/28/1910 San Francisco, California

Partak, Thomas Joseph, see Tom PARTAK

PARTAK, Tom 7/16/1946 San Francisco, California 94117

Patterson, Antonio Jemal, see Jemeal PATTERSON

Patterson, Carrol Anthony, see Pat PATTERSON

PATTERSON, Jemal 6/25/1969 Redwood Valley, California 95470

PATTERSON, Pat 8/13/1948 Los Angeles, California 90018

Paul, Joann, see Ruletta PAUL

PAUL, Robert Jr. 4/26/1977

PAUL, Ruletta 12/26/1953

PAYNEY, Lucille Estelle 9/4/1899 Ukiah, California

PERKINS, Irvin Ray, Jr. 11/20/1970

PERKINS, Lenora Martin 4/7/1913 Los Angeles, California

Perkins, Marcus, see ANDERSON, Marcus Anthony

Perkins, Marice, see ANDERSON, Marice St. Martin

PERKINS, Maud Ester 12/4/1949 Redwood Valley, California 95470

Perkins, Pinky, see PERKINS, Richardell Evelyn

PERKINS, Richardell Evelyn 12/21/1942 San Francisco, California 94115

PERRY, Leon 8/8/1917 San Francisco, California 94115

PETERSON, Rosa Lee 10/22/1900 Pasadena, California

Phillips, George Edwards, III, see George FORKS

Pierce, Linda, see Linda Theresa ARTERBERRY

Poindexter, Amanda, see EVER REJOICING

POLITE, Glenda Bell 8/1/1957 San Francisco, California

Polk, Joyce, see Joyce Marie BROWN

PONTS, Donna Louise 1/17/1963 Ukiah, California 95482

PONTS, Lois Agnes 1/21/1927 Ukiah, California 95482

Poplin, Oreen, see Oreen ARMSTRONG

Porter, Marlon Walker , see Dietrich WALKER

PROBY, Bessie Mae 11/23/1915 Los Angeles, California 90007

PROKES, Jim Jon (Kimo) 1/31/1975 San Francisco, California

PUGH, Eva Hazel 11/8/1908 Redwood Valley, California

PUGH, James Robert 3/15/1917 Redwood Valley, California

PURIFOY, Denise Elaine 11/4/1952 Redwood Valley, California

PURIFOY, Kathy Jean 2/27/1959 San Francisco, California 94117

PURSLEY, Cynthia 4/4/1956 Berkeley, California 94702

Q

QUINN, Norya 7/3/1972

QUINN, Ruthie Mae 9/30/1940 California

R

RAILBACK, Estella Mae 2/22/1904 Los Angeles, California 90037

RAMEY, Darlene 9/30/1959 San Francisco, California 94117

Randolph, Harriet, see Harriet Sarah TROPP

Rankin, Marie, see Marie LAWRENCE

RANKIN, Robert Louis 10/19/1939 Redwood Valley, California 95470

REED, Kenny

REED, Willie Bell 3/8/1913 Los Angeles, California 90006

REESE, Bertha Jones 4/18/1909 Los Angeles, California 90059

REEVES, L. Bee 1/11/1889 San Francisco, California

RHEA, Asha Tabia 1/27/1977 Ukiah, California 95482

RHEA, Jerome Othello, Jr. 3/30/1952 Ukiah, California 95482

Rhea, Pat, see Patricia Ann HOLLEY

Rhea , Patricia Ann Holley, see Patricia Ann HOLLEY

RHODES, Isaac Jerome 7/13/1971

RHODES, Marquess Dwight, Jr. 8/21/1970 San Francisco, California

Richardson, Kathy, see Kathy Jean PURIFOY

ROBERSON, Odenia Adams 3/10/1905 Los Angeles, California 90006

ROBERTS, Ammie Gladys 9/22/1900 Los Angeles, California 90006

Robertson, Acquinetta Evon , see Anita DEVERS

ROBINSON, Ben 6/30/1953 Los Angeles, California

ROBINSON, Greg

ROBINSON, Lee Ose 5/11/1919 San Francisco, California 94117

ROBINSON, Orlando Wemetric 8/1/1965

Robinson, Shirley Ann, see Shirley NEWELL

ROCHELLE, Anthony Eugene 3/30/1972 San Francisco, California 94102

ROCHELLE, Jackie 4/20/1956 San Francisco, California 94102

ROCHELLE, Kim Dwight 1/6/1967 San Francisco, California

ROCHELLE, Tommie Charlene 11/28/1950 San Francisco, California 94102

RODGERS, Mary Flavia 9/16/1892 Los Angeles, California 90003

RODGERS, Mary Johnson 1/25/1926 San Francisco, California 94117

RODGERS, Ophelia 12/26/1920 Los Angeles, California 90006

Rodriguez, Gloria, see Gloria Maria CARTER

RODRIGUEZ, Lisa 3/30/1966 Santa Barbara, California 93103

Rodriguez, Lisa Ann, see Lisa RODRIGUEZ

ROLLER, Edith Frances 12/18/1915 San Francisco, California 94117

ROLLINS, Dorothy Jean 1/10/1956 Richmond, California 94804

Romano, Marguerite Yvette, see Bippy DAVIS

Romano, Renee Sylvia, see Renee Sylvia DAVIS

ROSA, Gloria Yvonne 2/12/1956

ROSA, Kamari 3/7/1978 (none)

ROSA, Santiago Alberto 12/2/1954

ROSA, Therman Raylee 10/20/1976

ROSAS, Kay 6/19/1940 Redwood Valley, California

ROSS, Elsie Zilpha 7/15/1889 San Francisco, California 94117

Ross, Thelma Doris Mattie, see Thelma Doris Mattie CANNON

Rozynko, Annie Joyce , see Joyce ROZYNKO

ROZYNKO, Christian Leo 5/20/1954 San Francisco, California 94117

ROZYNKO, Joyce 6/2/1924 San Francisco, California 94117

ROZYNKO, Michael Thomas 9/12/1956 Redwood Valley, California 95470

RUBEN, Lula M. 6/1/1907 Los Angeles, California 90037

RUGGIERO, Elizabeth 8/8/1954 Eagle Rock, California

RUGGIERO, Roseann 6/12/1959 Eagle Rock, California

Runnels, Judy Ann, see Julie Ann RUNNELS

RUNNELS, Julie Ann 9/13/1966 San Francisco, California 94115

RYAN, LEO J.

S

SADLER, Linda Caleice 3/9/1957 San Francisco, California 94121

SANDERS, David Anthony 5/1/1969

SANDERS, Dorothy Jean 6/10/1947 Bakersfield, California 93304

SANDERS, Douglas 6/27/1950 Bakersfield, California 93304

SANDERS, Flora Bell 4/23/1910 Ukiah, California 95482

SANTIAGO, Alida Rosa 3/27/1958 San Francisco, California

SCHACHT, Laurence Eugene 10/2/1948 Redwood Valley, California 95470

SCHEID, Angelique Marie 10/13/1965 San Francisco, California

SCHEID, Donald Eugene, Jr. 7/22/1961 San Francisco, California

Scheid, Sophia Lauren, see Sophia Lauren CASANOVA

SCHROEDER, Deborah Faye 7/12/1949 San Francisco, California 94102

SCHROEDER, Tad 10/27/1973 San Francisco, California 94102

Scott, Karen Louise, see Karen LEWIS

SCOTT, Pauline 4/30/1921 Los Angeles, California 90006

Sellers, Marvin Wesley, see Marvin JANARO

SHARON, Rose O. 7/22/1907 San Francisco, California

SHAVERS, Mary Louise 10/19/1925 Ukiah, California 95482

SHELTON, Rose Jeanette 10/21/1902 Redwood Valley, California 95470

Silver, Penny, see Penny KERNS

SIMON, Aisha Kizuwanda 6/30/1976

SIMON, Alvin Harold, Jr. 10/8/1972

SIMON, Alvin Harold, Sr. 1/13/1945 Cotati, California 94928

SIMON, Anthony Joseph 7/22/1954 Los Angeles, California 90022

SIMON, Barbara Ann 10/11/1955 San Francisco, California 94117

SIMON, Bonnie Jean 3/23/1949 Cotati, California 94928

SIMON, Crystal Michelle 7/1/1974

SIMON, Jerome Mark 4/17/1958 San Francisco, California 94117

SIMON, Jose 8/20/1916 Middletown, California 94561

SIMON, Marcia Ann 10/11/1955 San Francisco, California 94117

SIMON, Melanie Wanda 11/7/1955 San Francisco, California 94117

SIMON, Pauline Louise 11/6/1932 San Francisco, California 94115

SIMON, Summer Renae 6/29/1976

SIMON, Zateese Lena 3/13/1978 (none)

SIMPSON, Dorothy Georgina 9/2/1922 Bakersfield, California 93304

SIMPSON, Jewell James 12/31/1921 Bakersfield, California 93304

SINES, Nancy Virginia 9/25/1949 Redwood Valley, California 95470

SINES, Ronald Bruce 2/18/1948 Redwood Valley, California 95470

SLY, Don 3/3/1936 Redwood Valley, California 95470

Sly, Donald Edward , see Don SLY

SLY, Mark Andrew 3/30/1961 Los Angeles, California 90020

Sly, Sylvia, see Sylvia Elaine GRUBBS

Sly, Ujara, see Don SLY

SMART, Alfred Laufton 6/3/1960 Los Angeles, California 90008

SMART, Scott Cameron 6/11/1963

SMART, Teri Lynn 9/11/1964

SMITH, Barbara Ann 10/6/1944 Ukiah, California 95482

SMITH, Bertha Charles 9/2/1902 Los Angeles, California 90006

Smith, Clark Andrew, see Clark GRUBBS

SMITH, David Elbert Vester 9/17/1926 Los Angeles, California 90011

SMITH, Dee Dee 10/4/1958 San Francisco, California 94117

Smith, Detra, see Detra Renee MURRAY

Smith, Edrena Demetria, see Dee SMITH

SMITH, Freeze Dry 1/12/1948 Oakland, California

SMITH, Gladys 1/11/1946 Redwood Valley, California 95470

SMITH, Hassan 7/28/1969

SMITH, James Alfred 12/25/1959 San Francisco, California 94115

SMITH, Jeffrey Dale 2/6/1971 Redwood Valley, California 95470

SMITH, Jerry Gilbert 4/17/1951 San Francisco, California 94117

SMITH, Karl Wayne 10/25/1967

SMITH, Klein Karats 3/4/1965 Redwood Valley, California 95470

Smith, Kelly Franklin, see Kelly GRUBBS

Smith, Kevan Deane, see Kevin GRUBBS

Smith, Kevin, see Freeze Dry SMITH

Smith, Kivin Earl, see Freeze Dry SMITH

SMITH, Krista Lynn 4/28/1966 Redwood Valley, California 95470

SMITH, Martin Luther 6/7/1978

SMITH, Michael Vail 7/27/1969 Redwood Valley, California 95470

SMITH, Ollie Marie 11/6/1959 San Francisco, California

SMITH, Shirley Faye 2/3/1948 Redwood Valley, California 95470

SMITH, Stephanie Marie 11/5/1964 San Francisco, California

SMITH, Vernon 4/23/1914

SMITH, Winnie Fred 1/11/1923 Los Angeles, California 90062

Smith, Youlanda, see Youlanda GRISSETTE

SNEED, Cleve Louise 8/14/1920 Pasadena, California 91103

SNEED, Eloise 5/18/1907 Los Angeles, California 90008

SNEED, Novella Novice 6/18/1907 Redwood Valley, California 95470

SNEED, Willie Delois 8/1/1919 Pasadena, California 91103

SNELL, Helen 2/28/1902 San Francisco, California 94115

SOLOMAN, Davis 12/23/1956 Redwood Valley, California 95470

Soloman, Dorrus Henry, see Davis SOLOMAN

Soloman, Shawanna, see Dorothy Pearl SOLOMAN

SOLOMON, Dorothy Pearl 9/19/1940 Redwood Valley, California 95470

Solomon, Syria Lesheena, see Tiny SOLOMAN

SOLOMON, Tiny 9/29/1959 Ukiah, California 95482

SOUDER, Delicia Jeanette 3/14/1972

SOUDER, Martha Mae 3/5/1916 Los Angeles, California 90002

SOUDER, Wanda Kay 12/17/1953 San Francisco, California

SOUDER, Yolanda 7/22/1973 W. Pittsburg, California

STAHL, Alfred Richmond, Sr. 7/24/1911 Ukiah, California 95482

STAHL, Bonnie Lynn 10/20/1970 Ukiah, California 95482

STAHL, Carol Ann 10/28/1938 Ukiah, California 95482

STAHL, Cathy Ann 3/30/1953 Ukiah, California 95842

Stahl, Judy , see Judith Kay IJAMES

Stalin, Jim, see James Joseph CORDELL

STALLING, Lula Mae 9/23/1924 Los Angeles, California 90006

STANFIELD, Donna Elizabeth 1/31/1909

STANLEY, YaVonne Renee 5/20/1975

STATEN, Abraham Lincoln 4/10/1912 Los Angeles, California 90037

STATEN, Ameal 1/7/1904

STEVENSON, Frances Lee 7/30/1916 San Francisco, California 94115

STEWART, Aurora May 9/17/1967 Santa Barbara, California 93103

STEWART, Terry Frederick, Jr. 3/21/1969 San Francisco, California

STOEN, John Victor 1/25/1972 San Francisco, California

Stone, Sharon Lee, see Tobi STONE

STONE, Tobi 12/13/1942 San Francisco, California 94117

STONE, Tobiana Johanna Dilorenzo 11/1/1969

STONE, Tracy Lamont 2/4/1967

STRIDER, Adeleine Mae 12/15/1904 Ukiah, California

Stroud, Daisy, see Daisy LEE

180

SWANEY, Nathaniel Brown 7/5/1922 Redwood Valley, California 95470

Swaney, Sharon Rose, see Sharon Rose COBB

SWANEY, Stephanie Kay 11/21/1966

SWINNEY, Cleave Lonso 4/5/1911 Redwood Valley, California 95470

SWINNEY, Darren 9/8/1968

Swinney, Joyce, see Joyce TOUCHETTE

SWINNEY, Timothy Maurice 9/28/1938 Redwood Valley, California 95470

SWINNEY, Wanda Shirley 8/20/1947 Redwood Valley, California 95470

T

TALLEY, Christine 6/22/1957 Redwood Valley, California

Talley, Maureen Cynthia, see Maureen Cynthia FITCH

TALLEY, Ronald Wayne 10/15/1945 Ukiah, California 95482

TALLEY, Vera Marie 2/3/1903 Ukiah, California 95480

TARDY, Armella 2/12/1946 San Francisco, California 94115

Tardy, Bernell Maurice, see Bernell Maurice HINES

TARDY, Eliot Wade 4/18/1968

Tarver, Darius, see Darius Daniel WHEELER

Tarver, Marlene, see Marlene Diane WHEELER

TAYLOR, Lillian Marie 12/7/1905 Los Angeles, California

TAYLOR, Lucille Beatrice 2/3/1898 Redwood Valley, California 95470

Taylor, Mom, see Virginia Vera TAYLOR

TAYLOR, Virginia Vera 7/29/1894 San Francisco, California 94109

Thomas, Alma, see Alma COLEY

THOMAS, Bernice 1/7/1910 San Francisco, California 94103

THOMAS, Carolyn Ann 12/3/1949 San Francisco, California 94102

THOMAS, Ernest 10/20/1919 San Francisco, California 90022

THOMAS, Evelyn 11/1/1944 San Pablo, California

THOMAS, Gabriel 3/13/1919 San Francisco, California

THOMAS, Lavonne Shannel 12/30/1970 San Francisco, California

THOMAS, Scott, Jr. 6/19/1957 San Francisco, California 94124

THOMAS, Willie Ater 7/28/1960 San Francisco, California 94115

THOMPSON, Etta 2/22/1904 Ukiah, California

Thompson, Samuel Lee, see Samuel Lee JOHNSON

THOMPSON, Vennie 4/3/1902 San Francisco, California 94121

TOM, Camille Tiffany 2/7/1976

TOUCHETTE, Albert Ardell 9/13/1954 Redwood Valley, California 95470

Touchette, Carol Joyce, see Joyce TOUCHETTE

Touchette, David, see David GEORGE

TOUCHETTE, Joyce 5/14/1933 Redwood Valley, California 95470

TOUCHETTE, Michelle Elaine 7/21/1958 Redwood Valley, California 95470

Touchette, Neal, see Neal WELCOME

Tow, Karen, see Karen Lea Tow LAYTON

TOWNS, Essie Mae 7/3/1903 Los Angeles, California 90029

TROPP, Harriet Sarah 4/16/1950 San Francisco, California 94117

TROPP, Richard David 10/9/1942 Redwood Valley, California 95470

Tropp, Sarah, see Harriet Sarah TROPP

TRUSS, Cornelius Lee, Jr. 9/20/1960 Oakland, California 94619

Truss, Dana, see Dana Danielle BERRY

TSCHETTER, Alfred Walter 6/19/1921 Ukiah, California 95482

TSCHETTER, Betty Jean 8/17/1959 Ukiah, California 95482

TSCHETTER, Mary Alice 6/7/1928 Ukiah, California 95482

TUCKER, Alleane 4/1/1929 Ukiah, California 95482

TUPPER, Janet Marie 7/31/1963

TUPPER, Larry Howard 12/5/1964 Redwood Valley, California 95470

TUPPER, Mary Elizabeth 12/16/1960 Redwood Valley, California 95470

TUPPER, Rita Jeanette 6/14/1933 Redwood Valley, California 95470

TUPPER, Ruth Ann 11/4/1956 Redwood Valley, California 95470

TURNER, Bruce Edward 4/11/1954 Redwood Valley, California

TURNER, James Elmor, Jr. 5/5/1959 Los Angeles, California 90059

TURNER, Ju'Quice Shawntreaa 3/18/1978 (none)

TURNER, Martha Elizabeth 9/23/1910

Turner, Rocky, see Lois Fontaine BREIDENBACH*

TURNER, Roosevelt W. 8/4/1926 Long Beach, California 90813

TURNER, Syola Williams 6/27/1912 Los Angeles, California 90016

TYLER, Gary Lee 8/3/1958 San Francisco, California

V

Vento, Celeste Marie, see Celeste DAVIS

Vezain, Rose, see Rose Marie McKNIGHT

VICTOR, Lillie Mae 2/2/1958 San Francisco, California 94115

W

WADE, James E Ford 6/6/1966 San Francisco, California

WADE, Keith 9/6/1961

WADE, Roberta Lee 12/12/1910 Richmond, California 94801

Wade, Terence* O'Keith , see Keith WADE

WAGNER, Inez Jeanette 12/13/1927 San Francisco, California 94112

WAGNER, Mark Stacey 1/7/1962 San Francisco, California 94112

WAGNER, Michelle Renee 5/18/1954

WALKER, Barbara Jean 10/25/1952 San Francisco, California

WALKER, Derek Deon III 11/18/1965 Oakland, California

WALKER, Dietrich 2/20/1974 San Francisco, California

WALKER, Gloria Dawn 11/4/1937 Inglewood, California 90301

WALKER, Jerrica Racquel 12/23/1970 San Francisco, California

WALKER, Mary Nellie 2/17/1904 San Francisco, California

Walker, Newhuanda Rhenelle, see Newhuanda Rhenelle DARNES

WALKER, Shawn 8/18/1972 San Francisco, California

WALKER, Tony Gerard 12/29/1957 Inglewood, California 90301

WARREN, Brenda Anne 11/9/1961 San Francisco, California 94115

WARREN, Gloria Faye 1/9/1959 San Francisco, California 94115

WARREN, Janice Marie 3/23/1960 San Francisco, California 94115

WASHINGTON, Annie Bell 5/24/1912 Los Angeles, California 90006

WASHINGTON, Eddie 7/27/1901 Los Angeles, California 90011

WASHINGTON, Grover 6/27/1927 Pittsburg, California 94565

Washington, Huldah Eddie, see Eddie WASHINGTON

WATKINS, Earlene Kidd 7/14/1907

Watkins, Erin Leroy, see Erin Jahna EICHLER

WATKINS, Gregory Lewis 11/9/1955 San Francisco, California

WATKINS, William Allan 4/28/1970

Watts, Olar, see Love Madgeleane JOY

WELCOME, Neal Shaun 7/10/1975

Werner, Darren Eugene, see Darren SWINNEY

Werner, Wanda, see Wanda Shirley SWINNEY

WESLEY, Bessie Mae 10/8/1915 Richmond, California

WHEELER, Darius Daniel 9/28/1970

WHEELER, Jeff L. 7/30/1965

WHEELER, Marlene Diane 2/11/1947 Redwood Valley, California 95470

Wideman, Ollie Marie, see Oliver Marie SMITH

Wilhite, Che, see Kennard J. WILHITE, Jr.

WILHITE, Cheryl Gail Gray 8/10/1955 San Francisco, California 94115

WILHITE, Janila Cherie 2/27/1974

WILHITE, Kennard J., Jr. 2/4/1978

WILHITE, Kennard Joseph 8/25/1952

Wilhite, LaShea, see Kennard J. WILHITE, Jr.

WIlhite, Nee Nee , see Janila Cherie WILHITE

WIlhite, Nini, see Janila Cherie WILHITE

WIlhite, Shanila Cherie , see Janila Cherie WILHITE

Wilkerson, Deanna (Diane) (Diana) Kay, see Deanna (Diane) (Diana) Kay WILKINSON

WILKINSON, Deanna (Diane) (Diana) Kay 10/19/1950 Los Angeles, California

Wilkinson, Loretta, see Loretta Mae CORDELL

WILLIAMS, Charles Wesley 9/8/1942 San Francisco, California 94115

WILLIAMS, Lisa Renee 6/27/1966

WILLIAMS, Louise Teska Lee 1/31/1913 San Francisco, California 94117

Williams, Ruthie , see Ruthie Mae QUINN

Williams, Siola, see Syola Williams TURNER

WILLIAMS, Theo, Jr. 12/6/1915 San Francisco, California

WILLIAMS, Tyrinia Tyrone 7/8/1970

WILLIS, Mary Pearl 12/21/1940 Los Angeles, California

WIllis, Melika, see Mary Pearl WILLIS

WILSEY, Janice Louise 9/23/1949 San Francisco, California

WILSON, Ezekiel 1/5/1962 San Francisco, California

WILSON, Jerry 2/14/1961 San Francisco, California 94112

WILSON, Jewell Lee 6/24/1929 San Francisco, California 94109

WILSON, Joe 6/29/1954 Redwood Valley, California 95470

Wilson, Joseph Lafayette, see Joe WILSON

Wilson, Shirley Mae, see Shirley Mae BAISY

Wilson, Wanda, see Wanda BAISY

WINFREY, Erma Merriam 12/19/1899

WINSTON, Alizzia Yvette 7/21/1974

WINTERS, Curtis Laurine 1/9/1925 Redwood Valley, California

WORLEY, Dorothy Lee 8/11/1914

WOTHERSPOON, Mary Beth 10/26/1949 Ukiah, California 95482

Wotherspoon, Mary Jr., see Mary Margaret WOTHERSPOON

WOTHERSPOON, Mary Margaret 11/7/1970 Ukiah, California 95482

Wotherspoon, Mary Sr., see Mary Beth WOTHERSPOON

WOTHERSPOON, Peter Andrew 5/5/1947 Ukiah, California 95482

Wright, Arlisa Lavette , see Lisa WRIGHT

WRIGHT, Keith Arnold 6/15/1962

WRIGHT, Leomy 5/22/1921 Los Angeles, California 90037

WRIGHT, Lisa 7/23/1961 Los Angeles, California

WRIGHT, Stanley Glenn 6/11/1960 San Francisco, California

Y

Yoon Ai, Kim, see Betty Jean TSCHETTER

Young, Elois Christine, see Christine COBB

YOUNG, Mona 7/19/1970